Pursuing the Mistress

Jean-Marie Nixon M.S.

DEDICATION

For my family and friends.
For your love, strength, support, and belief in me.

CONTENTS

In Appreciation

It is here that I express thanks to the many teachers, professors, tutors, and mentors who have helped and guided me thus far. I am still headed towards my final destination, and enjoying the journey along the way.

My first teachers were of course my parents, Earl Vernon Mills and Mary Louise De La Peña Mills, for whom, I can never fully express my gratitude or thank deeply enough for their support (loving, emotional, financial, etc) over the course of my lifetime. They taught me about faith, respect, and love. I would not be the woman I am today were it not have been for my parents.

I must convey appreciation to my grand-parents, Robert Mills & Maria Monrĕal De La Riva Mills, and David De La Peña &Irene Rodriguez De La Peña, along with previous ancestors. I cannot proceed into the future without respecting the past.

I wish to salute my sister, Cynthia Anne Sowers. She is an incredibly gifted woman, who shares so much of herself. She has often stated that I "have saved her life", but I believe that we perhaps have 'saved' one another (here's to you, little sis).

I cherish most and have learned so much from my astonishing children, Anna-Marie, Robert (aka Chuk Devlin), and Michelle-Anne. You are the joy of my life, and in teaching you three, I have learned more about life, laughter, and love than I could ever imagine. It has been an honor and pleasure to be your mother. As for my amazing grandchildren; Nina & Jordan; you two are the bright lights of the future. As for my grandchildren who are not yet here; well, I anticipate your arrival with joy.

I must also recognize three other wonderful people, Angel, Jennifer, and Zachary. It was not my privilege to be your mother, but I am grateful that you recognize me as 'your other mother'. I am blessed that you allow me to share in your lives. You are remarkable. I love you and your families. Your children are so very dear to me.

I want to thank my 'cuz', Robert Mills (who to me, is more like a younger brother). We found each other later in our lives, and I so appreciate our relationship. I have enjoyed our many philosophical and humorous discussions. Shalom, Bob.

I wish to thank the countless excellent professors, teachers, instructors, counselors, and tutors at Delaware Technical & Community College (both Terry & Owens campuses). It is here that I thank Mr. Charles Mundell of Student Support Services; I received invaluable assistance at the start of my academic career.

I must also convey my gratitude to the many exceptional professors, counselors, and support staff of California Coast University. I wish to particularly express thanks to Mr. Chris Stanley, the V.A. counselor of California Coast University; he was a pleasure to work with and offered guidance and support as I Pursued the Mistress.

In Utmost Appreciation

Finally, I acknowledge my loving husband, Patrick E. Nixon, who has been most encouraging throughout our marriage, my multiple career paths, the many medical and surgical procedures I have undergone, and especially, his support while I have pursued my master's degree in psychology. I treasure my marriage to him; we are like a fine wine, or extravagant dessert to each other. We do not require one another's perpetual presence in our day-to-day lives to exist or flourish. Many people will never understand our relationship. There have been numerous times throughout our lives when we have been unable to be together. Honey, remember this, you're always in my heart, never far from my thoughts, linked to my soul, and I will love you until the end of my days.

ACKNOWLEDGMENTS

It is here that I must thank the readers. It is my hope that this work is informative and enlightening. I am not writing as an expert in the field of psychology, but merely sharing my thoughts as I "Pursued the Mistress".

This book is a collection of paragraphs and essays, originally written as homework assignments. The collection is divided into sections which pertain to aspects of history and our multi-cultural society, environmental psychology, hazards of the helping profession, concerns regarding confidentiality and group work, and issues regarding testing and assessments.

I must also express my gratitude to all the sources and resources. I deeply hope and truly believe that I have cited all sources correctly. The information I collected has come from sources and textbooks used throughout my academic career. In some instances, I cited authors, who also cited sources in their own individual written works. I quoted some information from various areas of the entertainment industry as well. I have provided information garnered from various actual cases which I have worked on individually or in teams throughout my professional career.

There is no intent in this body of work to cause any harm (physical, emotional, or financial), or offense to any party. If there are any instances in this writing which cause harm to any party, it is done so unknowingly, without malice or intent.

I have learned so much while "Pursuing the Mistress". It is my hope that perhaps in this work, others will be inspired to achieve their goals, and not give up on their dreams.

Author's note:

I am a Hispanic American woman, in my mid-50s. I have had multiple career paths, & learned much from those I've met in various career fields. I have a disability; however, I manage as best as I can. I have my own "little cottage" business, which I enjoy, & often assist my husband with his work. I suffer from chronic pain due to an old injury & have had numerous medical and surgical procedures to my spine and lower back. I endeavor not to let my aches and pains get me down, as I try to keep a smile on my face and attempt to maintain a positive outlook. I believe that just because I am in pain, does not mean I have to be a pain. I am a lucky woman from a warm, caring home, with a big loving extended family.

The title of this book, Pursuing the Mistress, came about from a conversation with one of my physicians. I was speaking with her, and through the course of the conversation, I mentioned I was completing coursework for my Master's Degree. She then said, "well, the next time I see you, you'll be a Mistress, but not a head mistress, just a mistress". We laughed over this remark. The conversation would sometimes play around in the corners of my mind, and when I first toyed with the idea of putting the essays together in book form, the title just seemed to be appropriate.

CHAPTER 1

THOUGHTS & CONCERNS ON MULTI-CULTURAL ISSUES

A discussion of American culture as multiple group life

Before one can engage in a discussion of American culture as multiple group life, it is first necessary to define culture. In his book, "Counseling and Development in a Multicultural Society", John A. Axelson, states

> "I use a broad definition of culture. That is any group of people who identify or associate with one another on the basis of some common purpose, need, or similarity of background could constitute a cultural group . . . Most everyone in a pluralistic society such as the United States identifies with or relates to a number of groups, however the intensity and resilience of belonging will vary with each affiliation . . . The cultural base of a group is not a fixed or static entity but is constantly changing (transition from traditional to modern) in environmental interaction with other groups" (p. 3).

Utilizing this definition, one can say that since the founding fathers wrote "We the people . . ." the culture of this country was born on the dream and ideology of multiple groups coming together as one to "form a more perfect union." Since those early years, America continued to grow; immigrants from the entire world came and brought their languages, traditions, rituals, etc. in the hope of creating new lives while attempting to coexist with one another. In those early years, co-existence was more often than not fragile and futile at best. The newcomers defended their dignity and pride in an attempt to remain faithful to the old traditions. Along with day to day struggles to survive, the aspects of diversity, caused conflict. Conflict was often resolved with fisticuffs or gang violence. Alternate socially acceptable methods of resolution evolved through 'culture' – one of those cultures was sports boxing.

In the Lionsgate and Spike TV 2009 documentary, "*Facing Ali*", Canadian heavyweight champion, George Chuvalo states " Let's go back to the beginning . . . every race and colour [sic] that ever came to this country has shed their blood . . . Great Britain's Sir Henry Cooper said, "in the 20s and 30s you had the immigrant nations all going to America; that's why you had all the Jewish, Irish, and Italian fighters . . . you had to fight to make a living . . . nowadays 9 out of 10 are Mexican or Puerto Rican because that's the biggest influx into America. US heavyweight Ron Lyle adds, "the game hasn't changed – just had different people playing their part. Furthermore, US heavy weight George Foreman follows up with: "the left-right combination.

This is what built America (Derek Murray production).

Although this is not a discussion of boxing, this writer references the above quotes because they encompass the drive and determination of the immigrant population. These not only include the Europeans who entered through the side of the North Atlantic seaboard, but also includes the Asian influx from the Pacific coast, as well as, the Islanders headed towards the Gulf of Mexico, and the African peoples coming into the Mid-Atlantic, Chesapeake Bay, Outer Banks, and Caribbean waterways. Concurrently, other peoples were enveloped in American culture through war acquisitions, and territorial dispute, as is the case of the French Canadian indigenous people of Louisiana, and the Texans, Mexicans, and Mestizos of the Republic of Texas. All of these people of unique cultures brought with them their mores, and norms. One can recognize that the multitude of diverse peoples would indeed develop into a multiple group life. Politics and world events would continue to shape the nation and its citizens – individuals would embrace their "being American"; they had left the "old country" in search of a new, better life, and that in itself meant embracing change (in spite of the fact that change is difficult, it is the only constant in life).

The Americanization process had begun, and ethnic groups were strongly encouraged to give up the old ways and adopt the norms of the dominant majority. Anglo-conformity was strong and the majority of people transitioned into Anglo-Americans as this was the acceptable proto-type. Children were taught English in school and were encouraged to speak only English. Speaking the native language was not only discouraged but punishable. The message was clear, if you appeared, behaved, dressed, acted, or voiced anything other than what represented white society, you were considered "less than" – a second class citizen. Nobody wants to be second class in the land of the free. More often than not, assimilation was achieved by the 3rd generation.

The 1st generation, the grandparents, who initially came to America, still spoke with heavy accents and continued to speak the native language in the home and maintained the traditions. The 2nd generation, the parents, were bi-lingual; they spoke the native language to their parents, but at work and in social settings spoke English, dressed and acted American. The 3rd generation, the children, were completely American, they spoke only English (although they might have been able to understand the Native language), and absolutely accepted the norms and mores of the dominant majority. Anglo-American culture was entrenched. The "old ways" were out and this came about due to the power of the English language and the discouragement of using one's native tongue; because if "language is the bridge that connects us to other human beings" (Belsky, 1999, p. 109); then it stands to reason that one's native language would connect one to the roots of the native culture. The loss of the native language separated the 3rd generation of immigrants from the native country and transitioned them into Americans.

Nowadays the idea of multiculturalism is the more acceptable norm. People are encouraged to be proud of their ethnic heritage, and to embrace the traditional rituals of the old ways. This was in part to the political climate change of the 60's and 70's, the era of the civil rights, and women's movement. The paradigm shift due to the technological advances of the 80's, 90's produced an even more 'global mindset'. America and the American people are a microcosm of the world. They are a blend (some might still use the term melting pot) of multiple group life. The people are vast and varied in socio economic status, ethnicity, religion, language, sex, politics, and age; and as a people, have strengths to enable them to meet with the challenges which lie ahead.

References

Axelson, J.A. (1999). Today's society. In Ellen Murphy Editor, *Counseling and development in a multicultural society* (p. 3). Pacific Grove: Brooks/Cole.

Belsky, J. J. (1999). Sensory and motor functioning. In Jim Brace-Thompson Editor, *The psychology of aging* (p. 109). Pacific Grove: Brooks/Cole.

Murray, D. (Producer), and Jones, S. (Director). (2009). *Facing Ali* [Motion picture]. USA: Lionsgate and Spike TV

Ethics, several ethical principles

Ethics is the term used to describe rules of conduct. Most often, when the term ethics is applied, it refers to high morals, beliefs, values, and principles. When one states that an individual has a strong work ethic, it is implied that the individual is an ideal employee; a self-starter, their work is efficient, and requires little or no correction; the individual will often report early or stay later as required of the work situation. When it is said that a person is unethical, it is understood that the individual uses less than desirable methods to achieve objectives. In the helping profession, there are levels of ethical practice.

> "Mandatory ethics describes a level of ethical function wherein counselors merely act in compliance with minimal standards, acknowledging the basic 'musts' and "must not's" [sic]. Aspirational ethics describes the highest standards of conduct to which professional counselors can aspire and requires that counselors do more than simply meet the letter of the ethics code (Corey, Corey, and Callanan, 2003, p.12).

Ethical standards in the helping profession are critically important because the work is intensive and involves unique personal and sometimes traumatic situations. In, Corey, Corey, and

Callanan's book, Issues and Ethics in the Helping Profession, p. 13), it is stated

> Principle ethics is a set of obligations and a method that focuses on moral issues with the goals of (a) solving a particular dilemma or set of dilemmas and (b) establishing a framework to guide future ethical thinking and behavior. . . Virtue ethics focuses on character traits of the counselor and nonobligatory ideals to which professionals aspire rather than solving specific ethical dilemmas. Simply stated, principle ethics asks "is this situation unethical?' whereas virtue ethics asks "Am I doing what is best for my client?" Even in the absence of an ethical dilemma, virtue ethics compels the professional to be conscious of ethical behavior.

The counselor must be continuously aware of their own unique cultures. The first being the professional, the second being the personal (which is multi-faceted to include their specific race, ethnicity, gender, religion, etc). Experiences of both influence the cognitive, emotional, and behavioral components of the counselor. The positive synergy which can result from this rich intermingling may indeed lead to a higher standard of ethical professionalism, or eventual self-actualization. There are numerous professional organizations for those in the helping profession. A few of these organizations are the American Counseling Association, American Psychological Association, the American Association for Marriage and Family, and the National Association of Social Workers (Axelson, 1999, p. 64). It would be wise for the newly degreed and helping professional to become familiar with their own organization's code of ethics, as well as, the requirements of their specific agency. It is also important to remember the code of ethics does not answer specific problems to ethical dilemmas, but does offer guidance. It is up to the professional to examine the code of ethics, evaluate the dilemma, consult with colleagues, mentors, or supervisors (if necessary), and then follow up with the action necessary to confront the ethical dilemma.

References

Axelson, J.A. (1999). The culture of the counselor. In Eileen Murphy Editor *The culture of the counselor* (p.64). Pacific Grove: Brooks/Cole.

Corey, G., Corey, M.S., Callanan, P. (2003). Introduction to professional ethics. In Julie Martinez Editor *Issues and ethics in the helping profession* (pp. 12-13). Pacific Grove: Brooks/Cole.

Several features of traditional Protestant Values

Protestant values stem from the religious beliefs of the early Anglo Saxon settlers.

> Church going for the colonists was not easy. It was a rigid, demanding, and hard duty in the eyes of the 'God-fearing' Puritan people. Protestantism was the single belief system interwoven into the culture and customs of the society. . . Association with Protestantism as a means of psychological security was evidenced in the 1840s when fear of Catholic strength became especially strong and anti-Catholic sentiment was rampant (Axelson, 1999, P. 94).

The early settlers came to this country because of the intolerance in their native lands regarding religious practices, to avoid religious persecution and to be able to practice their faith without punishment. In doing so, they created social structures within their communities which were interdependent on one another and strongly rooted in their value system. One of these values consists of a strong work ethic. One's work and productive activity was a reflection of their connection with God, and that spiritual belief system led to greater self-respect which in turn created an ideology of positive self-worth and high self-esteem. This inter-dependency of faith and work was reinforced by the fact that hard work, and productive leisure time led not only to increased monetary gain for the individual, but also on a nationwide scale, this led to rapid economic growth. Individuals had a strong, deep-rooted belief in manifest destiny. Therefore, if one was faithful, and had a strong work ethic, one was accepted in society; this led to upward mobility, and monetary gains. Another value was that of self-denial; activities pursued for simple pleasure were frowned upon, or only pursued as a reward, but often times accompanied with feelings of guilt, because individuals were shirking their responsibilities if they were not actively working on self-improvement. Today, a strong work ethic is still valued, along with punctuality, dedication, conscientiousness, and accomplishment.

The following is this author's note of the protestant value system on society today:

Today, we also focus on the other "side of the coin". The strong adherence to Protestant values can lead to an over-dedication to work resulting in more stress. Time at work means time away from family which results in guilt at missing the important moments with one's family and friends. This can then lead to anxiety and depression. People who suffer from increased anxiety, frustration and agitation are then perceived as less cooperative and more competitive. This in turn can lead to increased aggression (as witnessed in road rage). Also, there is evidence of the increased manipulation of others in order for one to achieve one's goals or have one's needs met. The value of a healthy balance is missing.

Have we forgotten that other early historical document which stresses Life, Liberty and the Pursuit of Happiness? In the 2007 film, *Elegy*, actor Ben Kingsley portrays character David Keposh, a university professor, and author. In a scene, Keposh is interviewed about early American Puritan life; he indicates with the arrival of Miles Standish, America became a nation of straight laced Puritans and stamped out all happiness (1st scene). The early settlers wanted to pursue their beliefs without persecution, but on a large scale, they themselves were intolerant of others and persecuted and ostracized others for being different and having a different faith system. It was as though manifest destiny gave them "permission" to occupy a nation and its peoples, condone bigotry, and embrace self-righteousness. In wanting tolerance, they chose to be intolerant of others and individually became egocentric and as a nation, ultimately became ethnocentric – the Ugly Americans.

References

Axelson, J.A. (1999). Today's society. In Ellen Murphy Editor, *Counseling and development in a multicultural society* (p. 3). Pacific Grove: Brooks/Cole.

Luchessi, G., Lamal, A., Rosenburg, T. (Producer), and Coixet, I. (Director). (2007) *Elegy* [Motion picture]. USA: Lakeshore Entertainment.

Tracing the development of the Hispanic culture

To trace the development of the Hispanic culture, one needs to travel back through time to 1492 when Columbus and his shipmates left their ships and came ashore on the islands of what are now Cuba, the Dominican Republic, and Puerto Rico. The men comingled and cohabitated with the indigenous women; the offspring were labeled Mestizos, and the people learned the Spanish language. The Mestizos were the beginning of the Hispanic peoples. Later, Ponce de Leon and his men unknowingly landed on what is now the State of Florida; again the men cohabitated with the indigenous women. Once again, the result was Mestizos, with the Hispanic culture establishing roots in the Americas. The population continued to grow. Concurrently, the Catholic Church established missions throughout southwest America, Mexico, and the nearby islands. Thus began the conversion of the Mestizos to the Catholic faith. At the same time, the Spanish language continued to flourish and eventually became the native tongue of the people. Therefore, history shows the origin of the Hispanic culture with the landings and the eventual strongholds of the Spanish conquistadores; the establishment of the Catholic missions and subsequent conversions to the Catholic Faith; along with the increased usage of the Spanish language.

Today, the term Hispanic is used simplistically to identify a collection of ethnic people of different points of origin whose commonality is the Spanish language. Hispanics in the United States are mostly comprised of Mexican Americans, Puerto Ricans, and Cubans – the term "Hispanic" is also used regardless of whether one is an American citizen, a legal immigrant, or an illegal immigrant.

In the early history of America, the people were repressed and were considered 2nd class citizens. The Hispanics were expected to conform to the White Anglo-Saxon Protestant (WASP) values, norms, and mores. They were expected to assimilate into American culture and take on the attributes of the dominant majority. This did not occur because the peoples retained the Spanish language and in doing so they retained their culture, and traditions. This meant that the traditional mariachi music, and Spanish ballet folklorico dances would continue to be performed and taught to Hispanic children. The families continued to make the tortillas, tacos, and other Hispanic dishes. The Hispanic culture is a sensual culture with sensual people (this author does not mean sexual). All the senses are utilized and positively reinforced when one is immersed in the culture. The aromas and flavors of the different meals stimulates the senses of smell, and taste; the use of bright colors in clothes and the homes stimulates vision; the sounds, melody and harmony of the music, stimulate hearing; and the feel of different textures (woven serapes, delicate lace, pottery, and metal works) stimulate touch – utilization of the senses are continually and positively reinforced thus ensuring the continuance of the Hispanic culture.

There are several factors that were involved in the non-assimilation of the Hispanic culture to the dominant WASP majority. These factors are interconnected: the land, the family bonds, and their faith. A huge part of the retention of the culture was that the people remained in their land. They did not leave "the old country" as did the European people who expected a new start (the Europeans left behind their traditions as well as their native land and language, for a new beginning, thereby embracing the WASP way of life). The Hispanics were able to remain on their lands. (Author's note: I myself am 2nd generation American – my grandparents immigrated to America. My paternal grandfather came from Ireland; my other grandparents came from Mexico. When I am asked, "what part of Mexico did they come from", I say Texas; therefore, my own people were technically immigrants, but were here before Texas was part of America – their homes and their 'lands' remained the same – they did not leave the old country (everything remained the same, only the name changed). To better understand the "land connection" one must realize that the early belief system was that one did not "own the land". The Hispanic people had a relationship with the land – it was "*mi tierra*" (my earth) – there was (and in many places still is) a relationship with the earth – the land is yours to care for, and in caring for the land, the land will in turn supply crops, water, minerals, etc – it is yours to care for as long as you can – another common thought is "how can you own something that was here before your birth, and will be here long after you die". If the people left the area, they always anticipated returning to visit or stay (this was also due to strong family bonds). There was no severance of connection to one's birthplace or family.

In the Hispanic culture, family relationships are of the utmost importance; in fact, nothing is more important than the relationship one has with the people who matter in one's life. The importance of familial relationships is interconnected with their faith in the Catholic Church and their relationship with Our Lady of Guadalupe. Although not mentioned in the text, Our Lady of Guadalupe is a unifying force of strength for Hispanic people everywhere. This is because she made an appearance in Tepeyec, Mexico (their land) to a native peasant, Juan Diego, on December 12, 1531 – she appeared and requested a Teocalli (house of God) be built on this site. Eventually, a shrine was built. The Hispanic people love and adore her; individually they have a relationship with her, and indeed consider her their mother (Guadalupe, 1999, p. 501). She is the patroness of Mexico City and has been since 1737. The relationship the people have with her positively reinforces the importance of familial relationships among Hispanic people. The people acknowledge that she made a true appearance in Mexico, which added to the strength of Catholicism. It is because of these reasons, that the Hispanics did not assimilate and instead retained their own culture and passed this on to future generations.

In tracing the development of Hispanic culture, one must also remember that the Hispanic population continues to be the fastest growing population in the United States. It is also a young culture. "in 1989, 35% were under 18 years old and only 5% were 65 years or older, whereas in the U.S. population in general, only 25.6% were under 18 years old and about 12.6% were 65 years or older (Axelson), 1999, p 123). Hispanics have lower divorce rates and they tend to marry other Hispanics. Author's note: Here is an interesting scenario to consider-- If the Hispanic population continues to grow at this same rate, and the Hispanic people continue to marry other Hispanics, and if Puerto Rico became a state; then the Hispanic people will be the majority population, and the Spanish language will be spoken by more people in the United States than any other language. Should this ever occur, The US will witness a major paradigm shift involving politics, communications, etc., because of the huge increase in the voting power of the Latin people.

In continuance of the original question, specific factors: the retention of the Spanish language, the stronghold of the Catholicism in combination with the love and devotion of Our Lady of Guadalupe, the connection to one's birthplace, and the strength of family ties were the dominant forces in the establishment and retention of the Hispanic culture in the Unites States. These factors strongly influence the continuance of the Hispanic culture. Certainly, there are various sub-cultures within the culture (as with all cultures), groups within groups, all with their own unique differences. In spite of the differences, the Hispanic people are united by their sense of ethnic pride, and their culture remains alive, and will continue to flourish in America.

References

Axelson, J.A. (1999). Profiles of the American people. In Ellen Murphy Editor, *Counseling and development in a multicultural society* (p. 3). Pacific Grove: Brooks/Cole.

Guadalupe, M. Fr., (1999). The nican mopohua. No editor listed, The seven veils of our lady of Guadalupe: the new evangelization in light of the apparition of our lady Guadalupe. Goleta, CA: Queenship publishing.

A discussion of the historical relationship between American slavery and racism

Racism by Axelson's definition "is the belief that some races are inherently superior to others, prejudice is the emotional aspect of racism" (1999, p. 181). The term "slavery in America" describes a time in history when it was acceptable to sustain a racist attitude. During this time, the population of this country was sub-divided. There were the dominant majority, slaves, free people of color, and other minorities (the Asians working the railroads, the Mexicans working the lands, the indigenous Native Americans, etc). The slaves were considered property – they were not considered citizens, and as such had no rights. The sub-division reinforced negative prejudicial attitudes and behaviors. The barriers existed everywhere and it was difficult for all people especially if one was a member of a minority. The other free people were considered second-class citizens, but tolerated for their skills and labor; the dominant majority was at times forced to interact with these other people, but never the less maintained a prejudice.

The slave owners considered themselves superior to the slaves. While slavery existed, there was massive inequality – there was no system of power for the slaves – no schooling , no ability to own property, no vote, no way for self-improvement, and no way to gain a foothold into a power position. The slaves were oppressed by the white owners and the existing form of government at that time reinforced racism and prejudice because the dominant majority held authority and control over the slaves. Maslow's hierarchy of needs was not possible for the slaves, as their most basic needs had to come from the slave owners. The slaves were not empowered, many developed a learned helplessness; others developed the necessary ego-defense mechanisms for survival. The people of this country struggled through interpersonal and inter group conflict, thereby leading to the Civil War. History has shown through the Civil War and its aftermath the struggles this country has endured as a result of slavery in America. Racism and prejudice still exist, (as it has for centuries) and most likely will continue; the ugliness and its venom will not go away, but there is hope.

Authors note: Examples of these concepts (racism, prejudice, tolerance, hope, etc) are portrayed In Clint Eastwood's film 'Gran *Torino'*. The audience is exposed to the harsh ugliness of the racist attitude and prejudicial emotions of the main character Walt Kowalski. As the film progresses we witness his inner struggles as he slowly takes risks in acceptance and tolerance of his Hmong neighbors. He eventually bonds with his neighbors, and positive relationships develop. Towards the end of the film, Walt's 'white awareness' has grown very strong. Walt comes to terms with his life, past actions, and interpersonal relationships. During the course of events, an intolerable situation has occurred for his neighbors due to a heinous crime.

Walt intercedes and he ultimately sacrifices his life for the good of others. Our hope, as Americans, is that many citizens will continue to pursue efforts to overcome misunderstandings, and improve interpersonal relationships with all people.

References

Axelson, J.A. (1999). Sociopolitical issues. In Ellen Murphy Editor, *Counseling and development in a multicultural society* (p. 166). Pacific Grove: Brooks/Cole.

Eastwood, C. (Producer), and Eastwood, C. (Director). (2008). *Gran Torino* [Motion picture]. USA: Warner Brothers.

A description of the general features of the public education system

Axelson describes the general features of the education system through the emphasis of 6 concepts.

> (1) the systematic changing of children for life in the culture, (2) a nonvoluntary [sic] process, (3) relative isolation from other socialization groups and institutions, (4) a tacit link to other subsystems in the society, which exert pressures or constraints on the system, (5) perennial questions and issues that seemingly are perpetuated by the system itself, and (6) a complex maze of specialized roles and functions that emerge from what is thought to be an orderly and organized procedure (1999, p. 212).

The systematic changing of children occurs through the natural progression of aging. However, the change accelerates when a young child enters the education system. Most children enter the education system in what is known as early childhood education, some of these facilities are pre-school programs, Headstart agencies, or pre-kindergarten. The children are about 3 – 4 years old and are going through their respective critical growth periods; they are ready and eager to learn. The teachers in the classrooms are to be commended. The children are in small settings (as the teacher to child ratio varies from state to state), and learn social skills, cooperation, team work, along with colors, numbers, songs and rhymes, etc. The learning that they receive at this level is the catalyst for continued systematic change in the future. As children get older, they continue on to even more structured schools. The young children and early adolescents continue to change as their natural talents, and skills are further developed, hopefully nurtured, and positively reinforced. The young children eventually become adolescents and are funneled into more selective and structured controlled settings. Ideally, theses young individuals are experiencing positive, systematic changes. Either way, they are learning to adapt to their environment, improvise when necessary, and utilize the necessary skills to attain their needs and reach their goals. They do this while encountering other students of varied ethnicities, and cultures. They learn from observation of the adults (teachers, counselors, coaches, etc), mores, and norms of society. Schools are microcosms of society; children grow and change to meet their needs within these settings in a nonvoluntary manner.

Education is a nonvoluntary process. The majority of parents do not hesitate to enroll their children in school. Most parents acknowledge that reception of a good education will assist their child in attaining a successful career and ultimately a good, productive life. It is also mandatory in all states that children be enrolled in school, whether that be in an academic setting (traditional public schools, private schools, charter schools, and alternative education settings), or a home-school environment. Children's attendance is also nonvoluntary – they know from early on that their participation is mandatory. Some will make the best of the situation. Others love it, and view the education process as their social time broken up by classroom participation. Others will rebel and be non-compliant, and drop out of the system, or remain enrolled in school until they reach the age when they can legally withdraw from the system.

School settings are relatively isolated from other socialization groups and institutions. The majority of learning and socialization occurs in the school setting. Although, some educational institutions have memorandums of understanding with local police agencies, and child protective services, whereas, there may be an everyday presence of employees of these other agencies within the schools. Other than the small presence of other agencies, the schools are a world unto themselves. For the most part, the children begin their days early in the morning, often having breakfast at the school with other classmates. They remain in school throughout the day. They will have eaten lunch at school. Many students are involved in after-school activities (sports, clubs, music, drama, etc), so they remain at school for an even longer period of time, and often do not interact with their parents or other family members until much later in the day. This situation helps many parents who find it necessary to work long hours, or hold down two or more jobs – the parents know their child is at school; they find some sort of comfort and relief in this knowledge. Either way, many young people remain in individual isolated school settings for the majority of their waking day.

The schools have a link to other sectors of society. There is a direct relationship in topics and fields of interest being promoted in schools and speculation regarding the potential workforce needed for the economy. "Accomplishment in the system seems to be most necessary for adequate employment and socioeconomic mobility . . ." (Axelson, 1999, p. 216). This leads to pressures exerted on the education system to produce higher achievers, better athletes, more technologically advanced individuals. Unfortunately, the school system is burdened as the shortage of teachers continues. Other states are eliminating programs, and merging schools due to major budget cuts in this failing economy. This in turn leads to the question of self-perpetuation. The existing problems of today started decades ago, long before when there was segregation in the education system. Concerns for educational equality lead to integration, which lead to additional issues and concerns regarding student relationships. Teachers and counselors alike now had to deal with multiple stress situations and found themselves in the role of referee for volatile situations, diplomat to promote positive intergroup relationships, and advocate for the socioeconomically disadvantaged.

A huge factor for the Education system is federal funding (at the primary, secondary, and post-secondary levels). In order to receive federal funding, schools had to fulfill requirements. This put the system into a circle of events which lead to a self-perpetuation. The schools were already over-burdened with more students and less teachers in the workforce. This scenario lead to the need for more funds to attain the goals of meeting the students needs. This situation created more work to show justification for reception of funds (students must excel at athletic and scholarly tournaments, science fairs, SATs, etc). The cycle of overburdened teachers and stressed students continues exponentially across the United States. What develops is "a complex maze of specialized roles and functions that emerge from what is thought to be an orderly and organized procedure" (1999, p. 212). Everyone has a task or role, and each one, though independent, is interdependent on the other. As this writer views the major features of the education system, it is apparent that this is a microcosm of society as a whole.

References

Axelson, J.A. (1999). Education and achievement. In Ellen Murphy Editor, *Counseling and development in a multicultural society* (p. 205). Pacific Grove: Brooks/Cole.

Career development and characteristics

One of the factors involved in career development is economic trends (new technology, government legislation, fluctuations on Wall Street, etc); the dynamics affect the systems in which society exists. The result is constant changes in the workforce. The changes can also be attributed to natural attrition, world politics, population changes, etc. One theory which can also be applied to career development is supply and demand. Many counselors (Vocational Rehab, academic, military recruitment, etc) will advise clients of opportunities in career paths that will best meet both the individual's needs, as well as, the current needs in society. This is also because "timely career information that includes knowledge of economic and societal conditions can be integrated with a client's personal incentives or potential goals" (Axelson, p. 252). An example of this occurred in the late 90s in the State of Delaware; there was a shortage of nurses. Consequently, the State of Delaware offered huge incentives for students enrolling in College nursing programs. The State of Delaware also offered sign-on bonuses for nurses willing to re-locate to Delaware for professional career growth and upward mobility.

Education is yet another factor in career development – individuals must have the education and skills necessary for many occupations, and professions. "Deficiency in basic competencies (reading, writing, speaking, and computational skills) further impedes the acquisition of advanced education and skill training that are demanded by higher level occupations" (Axelson, 1999, p. 256). Education and the levels of education will continue to have an impact in career development. Recent years show that most racial/ethnic groups are attaining higher levels of education, while the proportion for White Americans has decreased at all levels of educational degrees (Axelson, p. 256).

Other factors related to career development are individual and group preferences. Many individuals and groups pursue either familial traditional occupations or gender-traditional roles. For example, it is not unusual for generations of families to seek career paths in police work, firefighting, or the military. At the same time, numerous family members may pursue careers in academia, medicine, law, etc. Often times, an individual's personal circumstances will determine a career path. "Social service work has attracted many people out of altruistic motives and also because there is real opportunity for employment" (p. 261). Author's note: while completing an A.A.S. degree in human services, specific for addictions counseling, this writer took two classes at Delaware Technical and Community College. In both classes, this writer was the only student that was not in active recovery. Many of the other students chose to pursue a career in addictions counseling because they felt they could better understand the clients and could help others because they knew first-hand the difficulties of addiction. This is just one example of how personal circumstances can influence career development.

The culture of people and the attitude toward career paths are also a factor in career development. Many occupations are associated with levels of status. Often times, jobs in the service industry are perceived as lower status, but are just as necessary and important for the economy as those jobs in a higher status category. Whatever one chooses to do, and where ever one goes, the majority of people and their individual career of choice are all interdependent on others and their respective careers.

Authors note: we are all just trying to make a few dollars, take care of our families, and make the most of our lives.

References

Axelson, J.A. (1999). Work and career development. In Ellen Murphy Editor, *Counseling and development in a multicultural society* (p. 238). Pacific Grove: Brooks/Cole.

Some physiological, and psychological responses to stress

Stress is that state of the body which causes one to feel uncomfortable, anxious, tense, and agitated. Additionally, stress can cause feelings of disappointment, depression, or passivity. It is often called the fight/flight mechanism which stems from the limbic system (This writer has also called this the fight/flight/freeze mechanism). It is the human response to threat, whether the threat is perceived or actual, and it is this response which leads to learned behavior. For example, many individuals (often with type "A" personalities) response to stress is anger (perhaps due to the feelings of frustration) leading to a volatile outburst. This writer describes the process:

The cognitive/physiological process provoking a volatile outburst

External trigger: This could be any number of things: heavy traffic, waiting on hold while attempting phone contact, shopping in crowds, etc.
↓

Physiological reaction: The Individual becomes hypersensitive in frustrating situation where there is an external locus of control, leading to an outburst → this situation repeats → further reinforcement with continued episodes.

At this point there may be a rapid heartbeat, which may or may not be accompanied by loud vocalization (yelling, shouting, etc). If the individual suffers from anxiety/panic episodes there may be signs of hyperventilation, if not, one can assume the blood CO_2 level is within safe range – perhaps loud vocalization prevents hyperventilating. Temperature regulation may fluctuate. Hypothalamus is most likely working at maximum capacity. Synaptic responses are firmly entrenched; oftentimes with little to no pause for reflection of action or consequence.

One can surmise that the body is flooded with the stress hormones adrenaline and noradrenalin; neurochemical substances that produce a burst of energy, a state of heightened arousal →the sympathetic nervous system "fight/flight" response. This prolonged response eventually wears the body down. One can only speculate the cortisol levels, although it is common knowledge that increased cortisol suppresses the immune system which may increase vulnerability to illness. Author's note: continual stressful episodes can lead to general adaptation syndrome – whereas any organism's response to a stressor occurs in 3 phases. The alarm phase, the adrenal cortex floods the body with hormones energizing the system to respond → the phase of resistance: output remains high and the individual is capable of superhuman feats → exhaustion phase: the capacities give out and individuals are drained, but could also become ill due to decreased immune functions

The psychological effects of stress are equally debilitating.

> Stress that requires adjustment to a situation or to oneself involves a relationship between the person and his or her environment. Stress occurs when there is an imbalance between the environmental requirements and the person's response capability, or between the subjective perception of demands and one's capability (Axelson, 1999, p. 296).

Actual or perceived threats can be harmful to the psychological makeup of an individual; they experience low self-esteem, suffer feelings of shame, guilt, helplessness. Other situations which may occur are disruptions of social relationships, which may lead to social isolation. The conflict situations which occur can be useful if viewed as an area of opportunity for learning new, socially appropriate responses. There is the approach/approach, approach/avoidance, avoidance/avoidance, and double approach/avoidance. Personality types are a factor in how an individual will learn to manage their stress. Type "A" will want to remain in control; they will struggle harder, become more aggressive, and view situations as competitive. Type "B" individuals will look at the circumstance and make the best of the situation. Type "C" will be inexpressive; this is the result of learned helplessness. With the counselor's guidance, one can find culturally, and socially appropriate methods for managing stress, as well as, look at life realistically, and learn how to meet life's challenges (negative and positive) in a healthy manner.

References

Axelson, J.A. (1999). Social and personal growth. In Ellen Murphy Editor, *Counseling and development in a multicultural society* (p. 205). Pacific Grove: Brooks/Cole.

Why the cultural history of therapy should be studied

The cultural history of therapy should be studied so that students can ascertain a better understanding of psychology, its theoretical perspectives, various levels of practicum, and theories of counseling. While completing their academic career, students can determine if they will pursue a clinical practice, seek out a career in academia, devote time to numerous human service agencies, etc. It is necessary to "know our past", so that we can be better participants in the future. It would also be irresponsible and unethical if one did not partake in this study. The psychology student, intern, novice case worker, or new counselor needs to know, understand, and internalize the primary features of the theory(s) which they are using in the field. Unless they have a thorough knowledge, they will do themselves and their clients a disservice. Whether they adhere to one particular theoretical approach (Rogerian, Glasser, Gestaldt, etc) or use a more eclectic approach, it is vital to have good historical, cultural knowledge of all types of therapies. The counselor must also have a good working knowledge of various personalities, the current DSM, and know how to develop a treatment plan. In order to best meet the client's needs, the counselor must assess the situation, ascertain a level of care, be empathic, understand that a phenomenological approach will be served if one develops a plan with the client, so that the client is empowered, and the client will support what they help to create. None of this would be possible without first knowing the cultural histories of the field of psychology and counseling.

Reference

Axelson, J.A. (1999). Traditional approaches to counseling and psychotherapy. In Ellen Murphy Editor, *Counseling and development in a multicultural society* (p. 352). Pacific Grove: Brooks/Cole.

A culturally specific approach to counseling

A culturally specific approach to counseling encompasses the value systems, social histories, and problems of many culturally different groups. "Because of the hostility of the environment and because of their cultural heritages, these (visible) minorities have maintained behaviors and values different from those of the dominant society" (Axelson, 1999, p. 410). In order for the counselor to utilize a culturally specific approach the counselor must have a good working knowledge of the clients cultural heritage (history in relation to the dominant culture, rituals, values, time and space, etc); recognize and respect the client's place (role) within the family, as well as, their place within the extended family or societal structure; understand the client's ability to recognize their personal problems, and how their personal problems are related to their societal structure. For example, when this writer was employed as a child and family case manager at an agency in Arizona, there were numerous Native American children served as clients. It was necessary to learn Tribal Law (as each tribe is its own nation and has specific laws dealing with children in foster care). This writer also learned and participated in "sweat lodges", "pow wows", and observed tribal races (which symbolize the enforced marches from the tribe's former lands to current reservations). In order to help the clients, this writer learned about regalia necessary for 'coming of age' ceremonies, etc. Another issue of difference is time; time on the reservations can be different from time in the United States. The attitude regarding time for appointments is often viewed differently as well. In addition, this writer collaborated with numerous agencies to schedule Child/Family Team Meetings to develop a plan of care to best meet the child's needs and ensure their participation in tribal rituals. This writer learned that the children belonged to different clans and together we explored their respective places within the tribe; examined the infrastructure of the tribal council; and most importantly, developed a plan of care so that this knowledge would benefit their personal lives. The children were encouraged to explore their feelings, communicate in a healthy manner, and practice techniques so they could better relate with others on and off the reservation. There were other events and activities involved in the care plan. The culturally specific and phenomenological approach best served the needs of the clients. A similar approach could be adapted and utilized with other diverse populations.

Reference

Axelson, J.A. (1999). Eclectic and synergetic approaches to counseling and psychotherapy. In Ellen Murphy Editor, *Counseling and development in a   multicultural society* (p. 389). Pacific Grove: Brooks/Cole.

Multi-cultural counseling: essential ingredients for the multicultural counselor, essential traits for understanding the client, and essential skills for the counselor in the counseling process.

Ideally, a counselor, whether one is employed at a private agency, government agency, school, health care facility, etc., has chosen the helping profession out of a deep sense of caring for other individuals and wanting to help individuals. Some essential ingredients are vitally related to being an effective multicultural counselor. A list of these would be:

1. Genuineness
2. Empathy
3. Unconditional positive regard
4. Strong sense of ethics
5. Courage and stamina
6. Creativity and enthusiasm
7. Having faith in one's self, and faith in the process
8. Respect for other cultures, values, ideas, and concerns
9. Establish trust and continually work on the counselor/client relationship

In his book, *Theory and practice of group counseling,* Corey quotes Pederson as saying, "in multicultural counseling, two or more people with different ways of perceiving their social environment attempt to work together in a helping relationship (2004, p. 15). The multicultural counselor must be open and receptive in working with clients. Additional traits for understanding the clients would include:

1. Know one's own cultural heritage and ethnic background
2. Know one's level of comfort in dealing with issues of oppression, racism, sexism, ageism, and diverse ethnicities
3. Encourage others to have pride in their respective heritage
4. Avoid stereotypes, labels, and narrow perceptions – transcend cultural encapsulation
5. Have a good basic knowledge of the client's culture, and be open to learn more.

A counselor learns many skills and techniques while completing their academic career. The counselor will acquire various skills while learning different theories; and are often able to practice different techniques while completing an internship, practicum, etc. The multicultural counselor would also utilize these methods, but would also employ other skills:

1. Be open to non-Western perspectives
2. Recognize the difference between resistance, reluctance, and polite respectfulness
3. Understand the fear, apprehension, and difficulties the clients may encounter on their way to meet with the counselor
4. Be aware of one's influence over others, and be able to 'look at one's self'
5. Be prepared for the unexpected
6. Create and maintain trust
7. Take risks, explore the use of culturally diverse methods
8. Don't be afraid to ask for help from "cultural colleagues" if necessary and appropriate (shamans, curanderas, elders, religious leaders, etc)

Working in the helping profession can be as rewarding as it is challenging. Multicultural counselors will utilize various ingredients, traits, and skills when working with clients. They will also use different strategies, and techniques to establish and maintain trust throughout the counseling relationship. Ideally, they will adhere to the ethical code of conduct, know their strengths and limitations, and find joy in helping others.

Reference

Axelson, J.A. (1999). The interaction of counselor and client. In Ellen Murphy Editor, *Counseling and development in a multicultural society* (p. 427). Pacific Grove: Brooks/Cole.

Corey, G.A. (2004). Introduction to group work. In Lisa Gebo Editor, *Theory and practice of group counseling* (p. 15). Belmont, CA: Brooks/Cole-Thomson Learning.

A discussion of multiculturalism as an emerging field

When one views the history of psychology, and reflects on the contributions made by Freud, Jung, and the many other notable scientists during the Victorian era, and then compares those contributions to the emerging field of multicultural and cross cultural counseling, it is impossible to be nothing short of amazed by the courage, wisdom, and commitment of all parties. At this point in time, America has existed since 1776, when the forefathers wrote, "We the People . . ." Prior to that event, people from various cultures were reaching the shores of America. The migration has continued to this day. In a popular song, Country singer, songwriter, Brad Paisley notes:

> "You know everywhere has somethin
> [sic] they're known for
> Although usually it washes up on our
> shores
> My great great [sic] granddaddy stepped
> off of that ship
> I bet he never ever dreamed we'd have all
> this . . .
> Little Italy and Chinatown sittin [sic] there
> side by side . . .

It's like we're all livin [sic] in a big ol' [sic] cup
Just fire up the blender and mix it all up"

When one considers that multiple cultures have co-existed together for over 200 years, it would seem that the development of this area of study is overdue. It is a comfort to know that people acknowledge the need for this theory and practice.

There has always been the desire to understand human nature, and there has been, in humankind, the inner thought of what are we here for, if not to help one another. It is this desire and inner thought or drive that fuels the multicultural and cross cultural counselor.   Foremost, it is necessary to recognize, and respect cultural diversity. To be truly good at this vocation, it is vital to be genuine, empathic, and have unconditional positive regard to others, along with remembering to "first, do no harm".

The novice counselor needs to acknowledge the significance of culture, and ethnic pride in their clients. These factors play a major part in the political and socioeconomic systems of the clients' world. The ripple effect and its ramifications are immense and sometimes surprising. For example, just as recently as this year's Professional Basketball playoffs, otherwise known as March Madness; the San Antonio Spurs beat the Dallas Mavericks. Shortly thereafter, sports announcer

Mike Bacsik posted on his Twitter page a racial slur, to the effect that he hoped the "dirty Mexicans" in San Antonio were happy over the victory. The aftermath was as follows:

> Mike Bacsik Jr., a former major-league pitcher who worked for KTCK (The Ticket 1310) as a talk-show host and producer, was fired Tuesday night, according to the Dallas Morning News. On Monday, The Ticket had suspended Bacsik for comments he made on his personal Twitter account. Tweeting on Sunday night about the Spurs' victory over the Mavericks, Bacsik blasted Spurs fans. "Congrats to all the dirty Mexicans in San Antonio". (KENS5 staff, 2010).

> But in a somewhat surprising development, San Antonio residents of Mexican descent have taken the controversy and stood it on its ear, in amusing garment form. Under a tent near General McMullen and Highway 90, a vendor is selling black shirts with the words, "Dirty Mexican." Above the "D" is a little sombrero. In the middle is the Spurs logo. "Everybody likes it, man," Javier Garcia says. "Everybody loves it. Everybody's wearing it. It's been selling out like crazy."

> Garcia told News Radio 1200 WOAI,
> the phrase has become a rallying cry,
> and indeed a point of pride, in the
> Hispanic community. "You can call us
> a dirty Mexican, you can call us clean,
> you can call us whatever you want,"
> Garcia said. "We're still going to the
> next round." That can be a metaphor
> for other things, by the way.
> (Chandler, 2010).

While this is not an essay about songs, or basketball fans, the above scenarios represent a tiny segment of the feelings of the American people and how the attitudes of race, stereotypes, ethnicities, etc, affect the psychological makeup of today's society. It is important for the counselor and others in the helping profession to empower clients to better understand and resolve their cultural identities, as well as, understand how their behaviors and interactions with others impact our society. It is also important to encourage all diverse populations to utilize mental health services if necessary, as well as, incorporating their own cultural traditional healers as so desired. Another factor which is necessary is to remain current in the doctrine; one should pursue further educational training (conferences, seminars, etc). One must also continually monitor oneself, question oneself, even be meta-cognitive about one's own values, feelings, knowledge of personal culture, and ethnicity. In the text, Issues and Ethics in the Helping Profession, Corey, Corey, and Callanan state: "Research has shown that counselors' values influence every phase of the therapeutic process. . . Clients are influenced by therapists' values and often adopt some of these values . . . In our view it is neither possible nor desirable for counselors to be completely neutral in this respect" (2003, p. 72). One must also have good working knowledge of the clients' religious beliefs, familial lines of authority and support, language differences, important calendar dates, time differentials, etc. There are many other vast numerous areas of consideration and opportunity for the counselor. Perhaps, this writer expressed herself best in a previous essay, when stated,

> Counselors, therapists, interns, and students in this field, who remain open-minded, and tolerant, may discover interesting personal and group dynamics while working with diverse populations. The exploration of another's value system can be a glimpse into deep intimate memories and moments. Clients offer the counselor a unique privilege and opportunity when they ask a member of our profession for help. We in the helping profession should do all we can to maintain this level of trust by being ethical, genuine, empathic, and offering unconditional positive regard.

Reference

Chandler, R. (2010, April 30). Re: Spurs fans embrace 'dirty Mexican controversy with snazzy shirt [Online forum comment]. Retrieved from http://outofbounds.nbcsports.com/2010/04-spurs-fans-embrace-dirty-Mexican-controversy-sith-snazzy-shirt.html.php.

Corey, G., Corey, M.S., Callanan, P. (2003). Values and the helping relationship. In Julie Martinez Editor, *Issues and ethics in the helping profession* (p. 72). Belmont, CA: Brooks/Cole-Thomson Learning.

KENS 5 staff (2010, April 27). Re: Radio station fires Bacsik over 'dirty Mexican' spurs fans twitter comment [Online forum comment]. Retrieved from http://www.kens5.com/news-Dallas-radio-station-fires-Bacsik-over-dirty-Mexican-Twitter-comment-92274964.html.

Paisley, B. (American Saturday night). On *American Saturday night* [CD]. Nashville, TN: Arista Records.

Chapter 2

Thoughts and concerns on environmental psychology

A description and discussion of environmental psychology and its characteristics

In their text, *Environmental Psychology*, Bell, Green, Fischer, and Baum, define environmental psychology as "the study of molar relationships between behavior and experience and natural environments" (2001, p.6). The term molar is used to refer to the simple sum of all parts, in this study, "all things make up one holistic environmental-perceptual behavior unit" (p. 6).

There are 5 distinct characteristics:

1. The emphasis on studying environment-behavior relationships
2. The environment-behavior relationship is an inter-relationship; the environment influences and constrains behavior, but also leads to changes in the environment.
3. Environmental psychology takes a given piece of research for both applied and theoretical purposes simultaneously – the cause and effect relationship and theoretical material evolve from the focus.

4. This field is part of an interdisciplinary and international study of environment and behavior.
5. This is an eclectic methodology – this draws on other studies, multi-disciplined, and involves multiple countries.

Environmental psychology is an important study for individuals to attain a better understanding of how the environment (climate, territory, density, etc) impacts humanity, and how people modify the environment to suit their needs. It is the hope of this study to raise the level of awareness so that people will be more socially conscious of their impact on the environment for future generations.

There are various research methods employed by environmental psychologists. The experimental method is one type of research that allows the researcher to positively identify the variable which causes the effects which one is studying. The experimental method is used in many types of research because the results can be measured. In spite of the positive results, this is one type that is not utilized often because "for environmental psychologists the liabilities of experimental methods frequently outweigh the benefits" as the degree of required control creates an artificial situation, thereby reducing external validity (p. 10). An alternate method is to conduct field experiments; however, these can be difficult to set up and can also appear artificial, and thus, reduce experiential realism. Some researchers are unable to conduct field studies due to control or logistics, and will use simulation methods; "by simulating the essential elements of a naturalistic setting in a laboratory, experiential realism and external validity are increased and experimental rigor is retained (p. 11). Correlation research is yet another method which occurs when the researcher cannot manipulate aspects of the situation or randomly assign participants. Correlation research requires careful observation of both the environment and participants to determine the relationship. "Correlational methods permit the researcher to use the natural, everyday environment as a laboratory . . . artificiality is not a problem, and generalizability – or external validity -- is greater (p.12). Descriptive research is also another method utilized by environment psychologists; this includes studies of what people are doing in their environment, how they are reacting to the environment, and what is their perspective of the environment. This also employs self- reports, data collection, observation, and task performance.

Preservationism and "deep ecology" and implications for social change?

Preservationism places emphasis on a holistic view – all parts of nature are interdependent on one another and a change to one system will affect other parts of the system; the intact system is greater than the sum of its parts.

Deep ecology is a form of ecocentrism. Ecocentrism or biocentrism adhere to the concept that natural environments possess value in their own right, independent of its value to humans. Deep ecology is a related and popular term which maintains that we are at a global crisis because our culture (technology, mechanics, and current systems) exists for the advancement of capitalism. The premise is that the human species is endangering the earth, and as a species, if we are to survive and co-exist with the natural world, we must envision and set about a major paradigm shift whereas, the earth does not belong to humankind, rather, it is humanity's responsibility to care for the earth, and its natural resources. Instead of competing with one another, we should cooperate with each other to protect and preserve the earth's natural resources for future generations.

A citation of several studies that support the existence of restorative environments.

In 1979, Ulrich conducted a study in which college students viewed a series of nature scenes -- this reduced the stress brought on by a college course examination. In another study (1984), he studied the effects of stress reduction on post surgical patients. The patients with a view of trees had a quicker recovery with fewer complications than did the patients who had a view of a brown brick wall. Additionally, in 1989, Kaplan, argued that "tasks that require mental effort draw upon directed attention" (p. 49). To achieve this goal, one must concentrate specifically on focusing one's attention to the point of not allowing any distractions, not allowing any expression of emotion, no intrusions. This exercise is of course is mentally exhausting, resulting in directed attention fatigue. The body needs to recharge, however, sleep is insufficient. Restorative environment is the key to 'reconnection'; it is a way for the body and mind to recharge, through reflection, relaxation, and rest.

Wayfinding: a discussion of several characteristics of physical settings that facilitate wayfinding.

In the text, *Environmental Psychology,* Bell, Green, Fischer, and Baum, indicate characteristics that facilitate wayfinding as: Differentiation, degree of visual of access, transition, and complexity of spatial layout. An example of these characteristics can be demonstrated through a description of the Jewish synagogue, the Temple Beth-El in San Antonio, Texas. Differentiation can be seen by its distinctive copper domed roof; there is no other building like this temple in the area. Degree of visual access is also quite easy for one can see different parts of the temple (meditation gardens, entries, etc) from various points of the parking lot. The transition is also simple -- Located just north of downtown San Antonio at the corner of San Pedro and West Ashby (very close to the major intersections of W Hildebrand Ave, and San Pedro Ave. The complexity of spatial layout is easily navigable due to simple floor plans, distinct tile walkways, and room identification signs (gift shop, library, dining area, meditation gardens, etc). Author's note: I have been in this building once, but remember the experience as both peaceful and tranquil.

Environmental load perspective: an example and description of each of the model's 5 parts, relative to the example.

The environmental load perspective refers to overstimulation and explains environment-behavior relationship. It can be broken down to 5 parts (p. 105).

1. People have limited capacity to process incoming stimuli and can invest only limited effort giving attention to these inputs. Part of this could be because all stimuli enter the frontal lobes where short-term memory is processed. An example of this is the divided consciousness which occurs when one drives, listens to the radio, and is going to a new address.

2. Overload happens when the amount of environmental stimuli exceeds the person's ability to process the relevant information. This would happen if the person driving and listening to the radio is in an unfamiliar area and hears of a severe weather warning. At this point, one would take a closer observation of the outside weather and perhaps adjust the driving speed to accommodate safety factors.

3. The individual will evaluate any additional environmental stimuli and decide if further

adjustments are required – the significance of the stimuli is evaluated by a monitoring process. The more uncertain one is about a situation, the more attention one will give the situation. Again we go back to driving and listening to the radio. If one hears that hail is striking some areas, one may make immediate changes either by taking a different route, taking a break, or seeking cover.

4. The amount of attention one can give to environmental stimuli is not constant and may be depleted after long demands. Again, one is driving through the storm, listening to the radio (for more alerts), while looking for an unfamiliar address. "This state of overload or directed attention fatigue (DAF) can result in increased mental errors, difficulty concentrating, and irritability" (p. 106). It is at this moment that the driver will lower the volume on the radio, so the driver can pay more close attention to locating the unfamiliar address.

5. DAF can be relieved through reduced demands on the information processing system, or through restorative environments. Once the driver has reached the destination, the environment is changed, and those demands on the information processing system cease to exist.

A description of several characteristics of stressors and of stress response.

In their book, *Environmental Psychology,* Bell, et al, quote "Lazarus and Cohen (1977) have described three general categories of environmental stressors: cataclysmic events, personal stressors, and background stressors (2001, p. 116).

Cataclysmic events are unpredictable, and include but are not limited to natural disasters (wildfires, tornadoes, etc), explosions, war, nuclear accidents, etc. There is little to no warning that the event will occur. The impact is sudden, and powerful. The response is universal, and great effort is required for effective coping.

In a previous essay, for course number PSY 507, this author states, "stress is that state of the body which causes one to feel uncomfortable, anxious, tense, and agitated. Additionally, stress can cause feelings of disappointment, depression, or passivity. It is often called the fight/flight mechanism which stems from the limbic system (This writer has also called this the fight/flight/freeze mechanism). It is the human response to threat, whether the threat is perceived or actual, and it is this response which leads to learned behavior (Nixon, 2010, p.37).

Because of the sudden volatility of the cataclysmic event, many victims experience shock and appear frozen. The gaze is can be described as the 1000 mile stare. They have witnessed too much horror and cannot process this information in such a short period of time. Oftentimes the severely threatening period is over quickly and if the stressor does not return, then people can begin the coping process. When the cataclysmic event occurs, it affects multitude of people at the same time, thereby, providing a large support system for one another. They can discuss their situations, feelings, and actions. This social support and networking can help the victims to better cope. Often times, the occurrence of a cataclysmic event will create numerous personal stressors for individuals, examples of this include the Twin Towers of New York, Hurricane Katrina, etc.

The second group of stressors – personal stressors would include situations such as personal injury or illness, death of a loved one, sudden unemployment. These events are also powerful enough to change the course of the individual's life. The initial impact is most severe, the victim suffers shock, the limbic system responds accordingly, and then the victim begins the process of coping. Usually, a personal stressor affects a minimal amount of people; therefore the social support system is reduced.

The third group of stressors is termed background stressors. These are not as sudden and powerful in intensity, but are more gradual, chronic, and routine. They can be classified as micro stressors and ambient stressors. The micro stressor is a 'daily hassle', such as, the alarm clock is late, the trash gets knocked over, the keys are lost, the bedpost gets in the way of your toes, etc. These are not intense or powerful, but are part of the stability of life. They are chronic in the fact that the events will continue to occur during the course of one's life (sometimes daily), and will affect each person in a unique way. The ambient stressor is "a chronic, global condition of the environment" (2001, p.118), and includes, but is not limited to, pollution, traffic, crowds, noise, etc. This represents an area of 'negativity" and the individual is reactive (as opposed to proactive). Ambient stressors can accumulate and create more stress for individuals, many times, there is not a point when the situation improves, and there is frequently no social support.

The major consequence of noise and a discussion of some variables related to its perception.

There are numerous consequences of noise (unwanted sound); among these are health issues (including hearing loss, decreased immune system, gastro-intestinal problems, and headaches), increased levels of stress and irritability, and poor task performance. However, "one of the major consequences of noise is a psychological one – annoyance" (p. 144). This makes people intolerant, miserable, upset, and discontent. There are "three major dimensions influencing how annoying a noise is to include: (1) volume; (2) predictability; and (3) perceived control" (p. 144). Therefore, loud, unpredictable noise, to which one has no control would result in a greater annoyance, seem more disturbing, and produce negative reactions. "Loud unpredictable, uncontrollable noise has the most deleterious effects on behavior" (p.145). Individuals will perceive noise as being annoyance if: the noise is either unnecessary or is perceived as having little value; the people who create the noise do not seem to care about the welfare of those affected by the noise; the person hearing the noise believes it is harmful, or associates the noise with fear (conditioned response), or is otherwise unhappy with their circumstances.

Several unpleasant and/or unhealthy effects of noise on humans

Noise can cause people to make more errors, perform poorly on complex tasks associated with vigilance, memory. Noise can lead to sleep deprivation, faltering memory functioning, poor morale, interference with communication, and decreased job performance. Moreover, noise effects social behavior, specifically attraction, aggression, and altruism. If one is to regard attraction -- when people are irritated by noise, it gives them something in common (they are sharing the experience of annoyance); and distorts the way they view other people). In view of aggression -- in his text, Bell et al quote "Cohen and Spacapan (1984) have argued that noise strengthens or increases aggression but does not provoke it. In order for noise to affect aggressive behavior, the behavior must be present for other reasons" (p.161). In consideration of altruism -- because noise makes individuals irritable, they are less likely to help others in need. Currently, studies are being conducted to determine if noise can be therapeutic – researchers are utilizing wide bands of "white noise", (noise used to 'mask" other sounds) to cover up narrow bands of unwanted noise. Further research is necessary before one can draw a definitive conclusion to this problem.

Jean-Marie Nixon

The seriousness of occupational noise

Occupational noise is a very serious problem; it is currently the second major problem in the workplace. This noise (particularly office noise) is a "wide band" of many different sounds at different frequencies and pitch. Consequently, it is very invasive, and all-encompassing. Depending on one's occupation, the noise can be very loud. Noise which is "above 90db, which is the level of noise produced by a heavy truck 50 feet away, noise becomes psychologically disturbing, and after repeated periods of exposure for eight hours or more, it can be physiologically damaging to hearing" (p.144). Currently, over 50% of US workers are exposed to noise levels which are likely to have an impact on hearing loss. How does exposure to noise influence interpersonal relationship? Cite research.

Noise, or unwanted sound, can cause stress, limit one's ability to remain focused, and affect behavior. As a result, exposure to noise has some bearing on interpersonal relationships by stimulus of attraction, altruism, and aggression. In their text, *Environmental Psychology,* Bell et al, cite several studies regarding noise. A study by Kenrick and Johnson (1979) "found that among women, exposure to aversive noise may increase attraction toward one who shares the aversive experience with the individual but may decrease attraction toward someone not actually experiencing the noise (2001, p. 159). In contrast, "Mathews, Canon, and Alexander (1974) found that even a noise of 80 dB increased the distance at which individuals felt comfortable with each other. Also . . . Apleyard and Lintell (1972) found less informal interaction among neighbors when traffic noise was greater (2001, p. 159). Individuals exposed to prolonged noise are annoyed, irritated, intolerant, and discontented. Their ability to focus is limited, and they experience environmental overload. It is no wonder that they barely acknowledge others around them, much less, concentrate on the characteristics of others in order to ponder the desires and risks of an interpersonal relationship. Another result of environmental overload of noise is its impact towards altruistic behaviors. Because people are already irritated and annoyed, they are less likely to help one another, because they either do not see or care that others are in distress. To further support this statement, in 1976, Cialdini and Kenrick, found "research in social psychology has indicated that being in a bad mood can reduce our inclination to help others" (Bell et al, 2001, p. 161). In contrast, research on noise and aggression has more decisive findings. Bell et al, cite a 1996 study by Anderson, Anderson, and Deuser, as well as, a 1993 study by Berkowitz; which "predict that under circumstances in which aggression is likely to occur, increasing an individual's arousal level will also increase the intensity of aggressive behavior" (2001, p. 160). Konecni, in 1975, found that noise increased aggressive behavior in individuals who were already in an angered state. Cohen and Spacapan, in 1984, supported Konecni by determining "that noise strengthens or increases aggression but does not provoke it. In order for noise to affect aggressive behavior, the behavior must be present for other reasons" (Bell et al, 2001, p. 161). When one considers that bombardment of noise causes irritability, annoyance, intolerance, and discontent, it is easy to visualize the transition of an annoyed individual (someone who just wants to escape the noise) to an angry, aggressive individual (someone who wants to destroy the noise).

A few brief paragraphs on aspects of environmental psychology

A very brief description of the major elements of the Gaia hypothesis.

The premise of the Gaia hypothesis is that the earth (as a single organism) is self-regulating in regards to its thermal process; this process is very similar to the homeostasis process in humans. In other words, the earth functions as a living single organism, and as such, has the ability for self-regulation, which is necessary for the earth's survival. Our planet maintains a spontaneous, and yet delicate balance which is interdependent upon the various species which inhabit the planet. Fluctuations between heat and cold occur naturally as animal, plant, and mineral life, the waters of the oceans, as well as, the atmosphere draw and release heat and emissions. The earth is self-perpetuating through its active feedback. It is all encompassing, and with a self-monitoring ecosystem has the ability to maintain equilibrium.

How heat affects performance.

Heat impairs mental tasks after prolonged exposure, impairs motor tasks after brief exposure, and may impair vigilance. Studies have occurred in the classroom, military, and industry. In regards to classroom studies, Bell et al cite, "Peplar (1972) studied climate- controlled (air conditioned) and non-climate controlled schools. . . in non-climate controlled schools, academic performance showed more variance . . . as temperatures rose. However, at climate-controlled schools, such variability did not occur on the warmest days (p. 182). In military settings, Bell et al cite, "Adam (1967) reviewed a number of British military studies that found that 20% - 25% of troops flown into tropical regions from more moderate climates suffered serious deterioration in combat effectiveness within 3 days and became in effect 'heat casualties' " (p. 182). In industrial settings, Bell et al state, "exposure to such industrial heat can cause dehydration, loss of salt, and muscle fatigue, which taken together can reduce endurance and hence impair performance (p 182).

What is SAD? What are some possible reasons for its occurrence?

SAD or Seasonal Affect Disorder is a cycle of depression. It is also called the winter blues or winter depression because, 'on cycle', SAD strikes individuals in the late autumn to winter season. The winter season brings shorter daylight hours and consequently less sunlight. "Experts are not sure what causes SAD, but they think it may be caused by a lack of sunlight. Lack of light may upset your sleep-wake cycle and other circadian rhythms. And it may cause problems with a brain chemical called serotonin that affects mood." (Web Md). "Lack of sunlight reduces the brain's production of serotonin, the mood-boosting brain chemical that . . . helps us feel happy" (Taylor, 2006, p. 69). The episodes of depression are marked by little energy, the need for excessive sleep, food cravings for fatty, high calorie foods, and weight gain. Some practitioners prescribe light therapy for individuals with SAD.

Author's note: everybody needs a little sunshine.

Do cold temperatures affect behavior?

There is little research regarding how cold temperatures affect behavior. Bell et al cite a few studies on cold temperatures. One study, by Bell and Baron (1977) found "moderately negative feelings associated with cold temperatures tended to increase aggression, but more extreme negative feelings associated with cold seemed to decrease aggression" (Bell et al, 2001, p. 192). In another study, Rotton found reports of fewer sex crimes on cold days. Bell et al state "informal observation has shown that cold harsh winters tend to increase helping behavior and reduce crime rates" (2001, p. 192). As of yet, there is insufficient study to show a positive correlation between cold weather and behavior.

Do the phases of the moon affect behavior?

It is a common belief system, among many individuals, that many aspects of behavior are linked to the moon. In fact, the lunar phases affect the tides. Similarly, some studies, have shown that lunar cycles affect behavior. "Lieber, and Sherwin [1972] reported a relationship between moon phase and homicide. Rape, robbery, and assault; burglary, larceny, and theft; and auto theft, drunkenness, disorderly conduct, and attacks on family and children have also been linked to a full moon [Tasso and Miller, 1976] (Bell et al, 2001, p. 198). Based on this information, it would appear that there is a positive correlation, however, other findings have shown that no such relationship exists, as previous research was skewed as it did not take into consideration, prior years research which negates this information. If anything, lunar phases and behavior appear to be self-fulfilling prophesies, as law enforcement, hospitals and emergency care facilities are pro-active; they have extra staff on duty, and are more vigilant to inappropriate behaviors.

Authors note: I will tell you a little secret that I told my children long ago: the moon is always full; just because it is not visibly full doesn't mean it isn't full. It is always there in the sky, regardless of whether it is day or night. Though the moon has no light of its own, we can always see it. I find it comforting to know that when I am looking a t the moon, my loved ones are seeing the same moon in the night sky.

What have been some of the effects of technological disasters?

Some of the effects of technological disasters are similar to natural disasters, such as the crisis effect, especially when the disaster is sudden and duration is immediate. However, the similarities end when the impact of the technological disaster is longer with lasting implications and complications. "When people are told that they have been exposed to toxic chemicals or believe that they have been irradiated, the perceived threat to life and limb" (p. 225) escalates feelings of fear, anxiety, grief, and horror. "People exposed to toxic hazards may have months or years to think about what is happening" (p.225). A fact that contributes to the stress is that people feel there is no control, unlike a natural disaster (where there is no control over nature); people feel they have control over man-made mechanisms and technology. Consequently, when disaster strikes as a result of a human-cause factor (Buffalo Creek Flood, Three Mile Island, BP Crisis In Gulf of Mexico, etc), there is also a sense of outrage, horror and betrayal. People will wonder, "How could this have happened?" Some will say, "Who are the individuals responsible?" Primary victims (people who are directly affected) will experience psychological difficulties, feelings of guilt of survivorship, anxiety, terror, nightmares, intrusive thoughts, and symptoms of post-traumatic stress. Some victims could develop post-traumatic stress disorder. Secondary victims (those not present at the time of the disaster, such as, relatives, absent property owners, etc) will also experience feelings of anxiety, fear, stress, etc). The magnitude of these problems is only increased by the constant everyday reminders of the situation in which people must continue their everyday lives.

A discussion of several ethical considerations in environmental psychology research. Do researchers have the right to observe people's behavior in the public domain?

In the practice of environmental psychology, the behavior of individuals is observed, noted, and measured. "...Many design and measurement techniques require that the participant be unaware that an investigation is taking place. This frequently improves the validity of research. . ." (p. 19). The ethical dilemmas that occur in this situation are involved with principle ethics and virtue ethics. Corey, Corey, and Callanan, in their text, *Issues and Ethics in the Helping Profession,* 'simply state, principle ethics asks "is this situation ethical?" whereas virtue ethics asks "Am I doing what is best for my client?" Even in the absence of an ethical dilemma, virtue ethics compels the professional to be conscious of ethical behavior" (2001, p. 13). This brings us to question whether researchers have the right to observe people's behavior in public domain. (Author's note: I often would tell my children, just because you can do something, doesn't mean you should – for every action, there is a consequence, and the choices you make today are the choices you have to live with tomorrow). Two specific areas of concern are (1) informed consent, and (2) invasion of privacy. Participants who are unaware of on-going research have not been informed and therefore have not given informed consent. They are unaware of the investigation and clearly do not have freedom of choice "Before unobtrusive field research is undertaken, an assessment has to be made concerning the extent to which human welfare and dignity are in jeopardy, and these concerns must be weighed against the value of the experiment Bell et al, 2001, p. 19). When individuals are observed and investigated without their knowledge it is an invasion of privacy, regardless of whether they are in a public domain. The argument is "since people in public settings realize they are under informal observation by others, most researchers believe that formal observation should be no more threatening" (p. 20). Researchers will justify their methods utilizing principle ethics. In matters of privacy, individuals should be made aware of research, and then they could choose whether or not to be participants. It is the opinion of this author that the ethical dilemmas and concerns regarding informed consent, privacy, as well as, autonomy, nonmaleficence, beneficence, etc, should be carefully evaluated and discussed with colleagues and/or supervisors before the onset of research methods.

Can the value of priceless natural assets be determined? A brief explanation

As I answer this question, I am reminded of the old saying, "beauty is in the eye of the beholder". Value, by its definition, is a numerical quantity assigned or determined to be a fair equivalent for something else. In regards to natural assets, this writer immediately brings to mind images of the following locations: Grand Canyon, Arizona; Glacier Bay, Alaska; Crater Lake, Oregon, Niagara Falls, New York; Bryce Canyon, Utah; Yellowstone National Park, California; Redwood National Park, California, and Sedona, Arizona. I suppose some individuals could and would place a value on these assets. In their text, *Environmental Psychology*, Bell et al, cite two studies by Clark et al, 1999, and Peterson et al, 1996. These two studies reveal that policymakers would derive the value of a

> forest in terms of its board feet of lumber and compare this with the economic value of managing the forest. . . In lawsuits following catastrophes. . . the courts typically use a method called contingent valuation to determine financial liability of those responsible. . . an alternative approach is the paired comparison method in which a panel selects the preferred item in each of many pairs of items . . it is possible to derive a rank ordering . . . from lowest value to highest value. Evidence suggest that people . . . do

indeed place very high values on natural assets (2001, p. 31).

Therefore, it would appear that the value of priceless natural assets can be determined, but for now, while we still can, perhaps we should just enjoy these resources. I know that is my intention.

An explanation of the dilemma of perceived control and ethical procedures. Propose solutions.

Individuals prefer to feel in control of their lives, situations, etc., (although there are some that would argue that control is an illusion). Therefore, in the event of a situation (weather, noise, crowds, waiting, etc) wherein individuals feel the loss of control, they find themselves dealing with reactance to the loss of perceived control. This is a normal occurrence in natural situations. The dilemma that occurs in research (controlled settings) is the guidelines which are in place regarding informed consent.

> Among these guidelines is a requirement that participants be informed of potential risks of being in the experiment, even though the risks are minimal. Moreover, participants must be told that they are free to terminate the experiment at any time and must sign an "informed-consent" statement disclosing the risk and the termination provision (Bell et al, 2001, p. 115).

Informed consent changed the subjects' perception of control, and thereby reduced the levels of stress. The ethical dilemma for the researchers (and no doubt a stressful situation for the researchers) was that they were unable to adequately study environmental stressors on their subjects because ethical procedures and guidelines eliminated negative reactions prior to the study. It is the opinion of this writer that 'virtue ethics' compels those in the helping profession to ask the question "am I doing what is best for my client". Is research, for the sake of research, in which subjects are placed in stressful, negative, situations justified. I propose this alternative – due to the fact that there are enough stressful situations in the world (natural and technological disasters, military situations, criminal elements, etc.); research could be conducted after the fact via surveys, interviews, collaboration with colleagues, etc. in order to gather facts, compile empirical data, and obtain information in the pursuit of the study of perceived control.

Some of the effects of toxic exposure.

There are numerous physical and psychological effects from toxic exposure. Physical effects include but are not limited to cancer, diabetes, birth defects, respiratory disorders, etc. Psychological problems include stress, and the numerous effects of stress, depression, anger, mistrust, and anxiety.

> The belief that one has been exposed to toxic substances, regardless of whether one has actually been exposed, seems to be sufficient to cause a stress reaction . . . the very belief that one has been exposed to toxic substances may cause long-term uncertainty and stress as well as pose a threat to one's health . . . however, the extent to which this occurs is determined by a number of situational and psychological factors (Bell et al, 2001, pp. 232-233).

A major factor which impacts how an individual will react to their situation is trust – if the individual maintains trust in the responsible agency, the individual maintains a more positive outlook, thereby keeping stress levels manageable. Another factor is whether one has a positive or negative attitude. This sounds very simplistic, however, Individuals with more positive attitudes tend to release endorphins into their systems, which help alleviate stress and pain. A large portion of anger and anxiety comes from lack of perceived control. People exposed to toxic substances have no control over their situation, thus resulting in long-term distress and worry. An example not noted in the textbook is the long-term effects of "Agent Orange". Agent Orange is the name of an herbicide used in Viet Nam during the Viet Nam War; many thousands of veterans still feel the repercussions of Agent Orange today. It has been linked with diabetes, cancer, hypertension, stress, etc. Veterans often refer to this as the gift that keeps on giving. Many veterans are not trusting of the government, but maintain a "warrior" attitude. They will keep on living as best as they can for as long as they can; not too many hide under the covers and wait for death. Their attitude is "I survived Viet Nam" or "what's the worst that can happen, they can't send me back to Nam".

Author's Note: bad things happen to good people, but life is about living and growing older isn't for the weak. I get up every day, and fight the good fight. I tell my family, you can choose to be happy or choose to be miserable, because the amount of work is the same.

How air pollution affects daily living

Air pollution is now and has been one of the primary environmental problems in this country. Every day, millions of Americans are breathing air which is contaminated with exhaust smoke from vehicles, microscopic particles from aero spray cans, factory chemicals, and emissions from industrial plants. Bell et al cite Rosenfield (2000) who stated "recent evidence indicates that air pollution actually reduces the amount of rainfall over a region" (2001, p. 239). "a report released by the U.S. Environmental Protection Agency in 2000 stated that since 1970, air pollution had been cut by a third" (2001, p. 239). How individuals view the problem of air pollution varies with their own unique phenomenological approach. "Perception of air pollution is also likely to be affected by factors of stress or annoyance" (Bell et al, 2001, p. 240). In 1987, a study was conducted by Winneke and Kaska; they surmised that individuals were less annoyed and stressed over chocolate factory pollutants, than by other factories, such as a brewery, tar oil refinery, and insulation plants. Individuals also view stressful life events as being related to air pollution.

A study of 500 Los Angeles residents over a three-year period found that having experienced stressful life events was related to more symptoms of emotional distress and mental health problems, and interacted with perceived pollution levels to predict distress

[Evans et al., 1987]. The highest levels of distress were observed among people experiencing stressful life events at medium levels of pollution. These findings suggest . . . people who are experiencing stress are more vulnerable to effects of air pollution (Bell et al., 2001, p. 244).

Air pollution also affects social behavior. "Asmus and Bell (1999) found that foul odors made participants feel more unpleasant, reduced willingness to help, increased anger, and increased flight behavior" (Bell et al., 2001, p. 244). Numerous studies have been conducted which show a positive correlation between air pollution and social behavior.

Author's note: Suffice to say, air pollution affects individuals' daily living because people perceive little to no control over this situation. This perception of "loss of control" can contribute to depression, anxiety, hopelessness, anger, aggression, and over all poor well-being. It is when people start to cope with their situations, that they attain hope, and see possible recovery and feel more in control. This in turn will give them a more positive outlook which will in itself become a self-fulfilling prophesy. The attitude shifts to one of: "I am going to do something in my life to make myself feel better, therefore I will feel better, because I will receive positive reinforcement for my efforts".

Space

A discussion of some functions of personal space. Is personal space an interpersonal distance continuum?

Personal space, or rather the invisible boundary we place around us, serves two main purposes: that of protection and communication. This ever adapting space protects us from being overwhelmed by external elements, when those elements become too great, as to present a possible overload on the senses. Personal space also aids in our ability to communicate with others. The distance between ourselves and others determines which senses we will utilize during the communication process. There are various factors which determine personal space: culture, ethnic identity, gender, and personality. All these factors are tied into one's comfort zone regarding personal space. If one's level of comfort with others becomes diminished (as in a crowded elevator), one's psychological, physical, and personal space will compensate accordingly, so that one's equilibrium is restored to an appropriate level of comfort.

Personal space is an interpersonal distance continuum. Personal space is not 'one size fits all'. This ever changing, shifting in size so as to fit the specific tasks at hand is what makes this an interpersonal distance continuum. The 'interpersonal' refers to person specific – there is no personal space between human and inanimate objects. The distance continuum is constantly shifting and rearranging as necessary to ensure equilibrium for the individual.

A description of each of Hall's spatial zones.

In their textbook, *Environmental Psychology*, Bell et al cite, Hall (1963, 1966) suggested that depending on situational conditions, people use one of four personal space zones in their interactions with others (2001, p 256). The use of these zones varies depending on our relationship with others and the current situation or activity. There are four zones: intimate, personal, social, and public. Intimate distance places individuals very closely, within 0 – 1 ½ feet. Personal distance allows for more space, within 1 ½ - 4 feet; this still allows for closeness between friends and acquaintances. Social distance is a broader space, from 4 – 12 feet; this would be utilized for business contacts and impersonal interactions. Public distance, of more than 12 feet, is for more public contact, such as political meeting, lectures, church sermons, etc. In observing, Hall's spatial zones, one must acknowledge that the zones will change depending on the situation, the culture, and ethnic identities of the people involved.

A brief description of a behavioral sink

A behavioral sink exists in area of high density, when the negative effects of high density are intensified. It is not unusual for behavioral sinks to exist in urban conditions where populations are high in a relatively small spatial setting, and personal space is minimal to non-existent. Personal space has a direct correlation on perceived control, and perceived control has a direct correlation to stress. This condition is a vicious and continual cycle. The over-crowded, high density conditions cause a loss of control, which leads to stress, which results in extremely negative behaviors, and less than minimally appropriate conditions. The cycle continues until stressors are so high that aggressive behavior erupts, resulting oftentimes in violence. One would typically find behavioral sinks in impoverished communities (methadone laboratories, drug houses, gang headquarters, etc.) and can occur in urban, suburban, and rural areas.

High density and the occurrence of negative effects

High density can cause extremely negative effects (severe negative physiological and behavioral reactions) to occur in non-human species; these effects are even greater when behavioral sinks develop. Studies on people demonstrate the effects of high density are neither uniform nor severe, but high density does affect illness, social behavior, and performance. Individuals need their personal space. Feelings of anxiety develop when the personal space is decreased due to high density.

> One field study had people perform a series of tasks in either crowded or uncrowded settings. It was found that they reported more anxiety in the dense than in the nondense conditions (Saegert, McIntosh, and West, 1975), although this probably does not surprise anyone who has ever had to perform a task with hordes of others "breathing down their neck" A study by Baum and Greenburg (1975) found that even the mere anticipation of being in high social density conditions causes a negative mood (Bell et al., 2001, p. 303).

Studies show that males have a need for more personal space than females. High density can cause physiological reactions as well. These reactions include increased heart rate, blood pressure, elevated cortisol levels, palmer sweat, and in cases involving crowded inmates, there was an increased level of urinary catecholamines. Consequently, it is not surprising that high density can lead to poor health and "contribute to illness due to stress, also . . . disease can spread more quickly" (Bell et al., 2001, P. 305).

Social behavior is also affected by high density. Bell et al, cite Baum and Greenberg in stating, "the mere expectation of high social density elicits withdrawal responses, including lower levels of eye contact, head movements away from others . . .and maintenance of greater interpersonal distance (2001, p. 307). High density impacts social behavior because people distance themselves from one another, thereby breaking down the social supportive network that is essential for helping individuals to cope with stressful life events. "In studies that explored how helping is affected by building density, it was found that greater density leads to less helping (Bell et al., 2001, p. 309). As a result, one could rationalize that high density leads to hurtful behavior. "Subsequent research . . . has shown increases in aggression under conditions of very high social density in boys" (Bell et al., 2001, P 310). "Often, it appears that increased density leads to aggression in adult males but not in females, a familiar pattern in high density research (Bell et al., 2001, p. 310). In regards to the effects of high density on task performance, the results are varied. Early studies show no decrease in performance occurring in both high social and spatial density when individuals performed simple easy tasks. Later, studies which involved more complex tasks showed that both high social and spatial density led to decreased performance. While later still, other studies showed contradictions depending on social or special density and the complexity of the tasks. It may be considered that perceived control has bearing in the situation and results in a self-fulfilling prophesy. Schkade in 1978, studied task behavior, wherein she manipulated spatial density and the expectancy of performance by individuals. "Results showed that the poorest task performance occurred when density was high and expectations were low – that is people did not expect to do well on the task" (Bell et al., 2001, p. 313). It would appear that when individuals feel better in regards to their health, they tend to behave better with one another. They also perform better on tasks when they have adequate personal space, or their perception of personal space is optimal.

Author's note – a little elbow room can go a long way.

A summarization of the research on the negative effects of urban life on the city dweller.

There has been varied research on the negative effects of living in cities. Most people will concur that cities have more crime, pollution, and traffic; this can lead to great stress on individuals. Cities, by the fact that there is a higher density of population in less spatial settings, produce great stressors to include crowding, less prosocial behavior, and crime. Crowding leads to bombardment of the senses and more tension in everyday life. A 1974 study by Franck, Unseld, and Wentworth, showed that "urban newcomers reported experiencing significantly more tension when living in the city than in their previous residence; the reverse was observed for rural newcomers" (Bell et al, 2001, p. 340). Another source of stress and tension is the feeling of being alone. In two separate studies, it was evident that individuals living in two different cities, showed less eye contact and less affiliative behavior than those individuals living in small towns. One can speculate that in spite of living where there are hundreds of thousands of people, perhaps even millions, one often feels alone. These findings also extend to prosocial behavior. Milgram discovered, in 1977, "when a child claiming to be lost asked for aid in New York City and in several small towns, he or she was more likely to be the recipient of prosocial (helping) behavior in the smaller towns" (Bell et al., 2001, p. 342). It is to be noted that Stebly, in 1987, found that helping behavior decreases in "communities with a population of 300,000 or more (Bell et al., 2110, p. 342), and "according to Levine et al., (1994), population density . . . is more likely to be related to unhelpful behavior than population size". There are a number of theories as to why city dwellers are more unwilling to help, such as sensory overload, the personal insecurities of individuals, "urban personality" which is not predisposed to help, and **diffusion of responsibility.** "Work on diffusion of responsibility suggests that when there are many people around who could help (as would occur more in cities than in small towns), perceived responsibility to help lessens, which affects the likelihood of giving aid" (Bell et al;, 2001, p. 343). It is not surprising that a person will feel alone among hundreds of thousands of people. Another source of stress is crime. Bell et al., in 1998, quote information from the U. S. Census Bureau, "the rate of violent crimes per person is almost six times greater in the large metropolitan cities than in rural areas" (2001, p. 344). Zimbardo, in 1969, theorized a reason for more crime in cities as **deindividuation.** "According to this theory, when we feel as we are an anonymous member of a crowd (i.e. deindividuation), our inhibitions against antisocial behavior are released. This is partly because we feel it is very unlikely that we will be identified and punished" (Bell, et al., 2001, p. 345). Of course, there are other factors for higher crime, such as unemployment, perceived inequity, fewer role models, and there are more opportunities for crime because there are more possible victims. As a result, the research substantiates the negative effects on those living in large cities.

Some environmental solutions to urban problems

Due to the numerous negative effects on city dwellers, it is not surprising that many people relocate to the suburbs, and rural areas. As a result, the population of cities declines and leaves the cities in fading conditions due to a decreased tax base, unemployment, and increased social problems. In order for cities to remain alive, people must continue to support "city life", whether for social, financial, or spiritual reasons. Some venues for this would be attractions, such as theaters, museums, arboretums, shopping centers, cathedrals, parks, etc. It is to be noted that the presence of trees and grassy areas (maintained, landscaped areas) fosters feelings of safety among individuals. Bell et al., quote Taylor, Wiley, Kuo, and Sullivan from a 1998 "study of inner-city children and outdoor spaces, it was found that level of play, supervision by adults, and creativity in play were approximately doubled in areas with green grass and trees compared with barren areas" (2001, P. 348). Many cities today have open parks with waterways to provide a natural outlet for individuals. A few most notable parks are Central Park in New York City, Golden Gate Park in San Francisco, and the "Mall" in Washington, D.C. These areas provide people the "opportunity to breathe", temporarily escape from the stressors of the cities, while being able to spend quality time with their families. Other outdoor settings, which offer respite from the stressors of city life, are urban gardens and playgrounds. Urban renewal and restoring existing residential neighborhoods are also other means of solving urban problems. Many neighbors form strong social networks and block organizations. These groups provide a sense of community, and

> could play a significant role in fostering the ability to cope with urban problems. The presence of social networks helps regulate access to an area by strangers, leads to less reliance on police for dealing with disturbances, and reduces the need for a "get tough" policy by police when their help is required (Frug, 1999; Taylor, 1988). . . "Neighboring" in urban environments is greater when there is ethnic similarity, shared socioeconomic status, psychological "investment" in a neighborhood, satisfaction with conditions there, and a positive sense of well-being (Bell et al., 2001, p. 358).

Still other solutions for urban problems include revitalizing business districts, creating festival marketplaces, and pedestrian plazas or pedestrian malls. "The idea is to reduce traffic congestion, beautify the area, and encourage commerce in previously deteriorating areas . . . pedestrian plazas can liven up the environment. Food vendors, sunny areas, places to sit, and fountains promote the habitability of such spaces" (Bell et al., 2001, p. 364). The research indicates that environmental solutions to urban problems consist of utilizing nature (trees, foliage, water, birdsong, etc); in doing so, the senses are pleasantly stimulated, and individuals can escape from the stressors of urban troubles and tribulations.

Author's note: a little bit of nature is like a little slice of heaven.

Several theoretical perspectives on crowding along with a description of the causes of crowding and the primary coping mechanisms.

As per Bell, et al., there are numerous theoretical perspectives on crowding. One approach is social overload due to excessive social stimuli (too much social contact), coping mechanisms include escape from the stimuli either through withdrawal, or by prioritizing one's commitments and avoiding low priorities (this is often evident during the holiday season, and is one reason people are often exhausted from attending many holiday events). Another perspective is behavioral constraint caused by a reduction of behavioral freedom; the coping mechanisms could include aggressive behavior, leaving the situation, or coordinating one's actions with others (this is most evident in children's behaviors at reunions. They are already over stimulated, stressed because they know they need to be on their best behavior, get frustrated and act out. Parents may have strategized prior to the event and plan accordingly, or they have the option of leaving the reunion). Also, there is the ecological perspective caused by scarcity of resources. The primary coping mechanism is the defense of group boundaries and exclusion of outsiders. This is evident in areas of the southwestern United States where water is a scarce and precious resource. Cities and communities are established in areas close to water, and sometimes water is rationed to the residents. Next, there is the perspective of unwanted interaction caused by excessive, unwanted interaction with others (which can lead to stress); the coping method is withdrawal or organization into smaller groups. Last of all, there is the concept of privacy regulation; crowding can lead to minimal privacy; people cope by utilizing more privacy control methods.

Person-environment congruence and its importance

The term person-environment congruence indicates that a person(s) and their immediate environment must be in congruence for the most positive and successful outcomes to occur. It is important because (1) "the setting facilitates the behaviors and goals appropriate to the setting" (Bell et al., 2001, p. 400); a restaurant setting is where individuals go to have a pleasant dining experience, and churches are places people visit for spiritual worship; the environment and behaviors of those in the environment are congruent; and (2) it is also a matter of perceived control; "our behavior in the setting is in part a function of the degree of perceived control the environment offers" (Bell et al., 2001, p. 401). Individuals who maintain more perceived control of their environment will feel less constrained. "The term constraint means that something about the environment is limiting or interfering with things we wish to do" (Bell et al, 2001, p, 113). Individuals in a library or more apt to be quiet, observe appropriate social boundaries, and be aware of one another's personal space because of person-environment congruence, but also because their perception of control within the library is appropriate to the library setting.

Space in institutional environments and how this contributes to interaction

Institutional environments differ from residential environments in that they are shared with more people, therefore, there is less privacy, as well as, less perceived control. People are also less territorial in institutional settings, and overstimulation is also quite common. Hospital settings and psychiatric facilities are institutional settings in which patients have minimal or no control over the allotted space. However, "designs that protect privacy yet encourage appropriate social interaction seem to be the most therapeutic" (Bell et al., 2001, p. 416). It can also be noted that specific placement of furniture can encourage people to interact with one another. Bell et al. cite Cherulnik's 1993 study of institutional layouts. In one study,

> a corridor design and suite design were compared with a control condition in which the previous institutional layout was unchanged. In the corridor design, one to two residents lived in each room with floor to ceiling walls and lockable doors. In suite design, one to three residents were housed per room, with partitions used to separate sleeping areas and homelike furnishings supplied. Residents appeared most alert and purposive and interacted most with other residents (and less with staff) in the suite design. . . In another case, dormitories were partitioned into two room modules . . . chairs were arranged in a semicircle sociopetal

configuration. Social interaction among the residents doubled after design modification (2001, p. 419).

In regard to prison designs, "grouping prisoner together in large numbers is less healthful than grouping them together in small numbers, and single- or double-occupancy cells are better . . . than cells with more prisoners (Bell et al., 2001, p. 420). Bell et al. go on further to state "new prison designs . . . attempt to provide more 'humane' environments . . . with natural barriers . . . color and lighting . . . and increasing opportunities for privacy by providing more single-occupancy cells and designing windows so narrow they do not need bars" (2001, p. 421). In addition, "rather than separate observational booths or rooms for guards, the guards are placed directly in the living quarters of the inmates to increase interaction" (2001, p. 421).

In nursing home situations, a new approach design referred to as "the Eden Alternative" has had positive results among dementia and non-dementia residents. "This institutional unit . . contains dozens of animals . . . and hundreds of plants for the residents to observe, care for, and handle. . . This opportunity to 'commune with nature' can be very therapeutic" (Bell et al., 2001, p. 428). It is evident from research and studies that increased interaction results from designs that allow for a certain amount of privacy, utilize existing space for smaller groups, incorporate natural items such as plants and animals, and allow arrangement of furniture for more social conditions.

Territoriality in work environments

One can view territory as a place that is either owned or controlled by one or others. Bell et al., state "human territoriality can be viewed as a set of behaviors and cognitions a person or group exhibits, based on perceived ownership of physical space" (2001, p. 276). In work environments, territories can be viewed as an individual's assigned work equipment, or a person's office area. This concept is sometimes referred to as the 'assigned workspace' or 'fixed workspace'. Bell et al., cite Sundstrom's 1986 work, in which he "suggests that the right to treat a workspace as a territory might lead to more personal attachment to it, more perceived control over it, and thus more sense of personalization of the workspace" (2001, p. 438). One can also acknowledge that in work environments where there is considerable office space, territories may be seen as status symbols. The territory may be a bigger office, or an area with a view. In this manner, the status symbol reflects power, advancement, and /or authority. Sundstrom, in 1986, also said the territorial status symbol "communicate status and power to others, they compensate employees as a nonmonetary benefit, and they serve as props or tools (such as larger desks, filing cabinets, computer terminals), which the worker is privileged to use on the job" (Bell et al., 2001, p. 438). Furthermore, Konar et al., in 1982, state "the more one can attach status to the office space, the more satisfied one is with the job" (Bell et al., 2001, p. 439).

It is the opinion of this writer that office workers who are able to adjust their office space or cubicles to fit their needs, set up their 'desk area', and decorate their spaces as they desire perform better in the work environment, as a result of perceived control and person-environment congruence.

Personalization and how this varies with status, gender, age, or career

Personalization varies accordingly to one's personality. "Since personality represents one's way of looking at the world and reflects learning and experience, it seems reasonable that personality orientations should be reflected in spatial behavior (Bell et al., 2001, p. 261). Similarly, it would seem reasonable that personalization will vary with status, career, gender, and age, and one would also see variances in personal space. Bell et al., state "the ability to treat a workspace as a territory, to adjust it, and to personalize it serves as a form of status and may increase job satisfaction, especially at higher ranks in the organization (2001, p. 447). They also cite a study by Fahriye Sancar and Baris Eyikan in 1995 in which they "surveyed studio instructors of architecture and landscape architecture at more than 60 schools in the United States. They concluded ' . . .the professional identity of designers is being transformed from that of isolated creative individuals to that of politically active professionals' (Bell et al., 2001, p. 383). One would summarize that as the students became confident in their skills, their work would demonstrate personalization (in this case politically active professionals). In regards to gender, Aiello, 1987; Barnard and Bell 1982 studied gender differences in personal space; the finding show "in terms of same-sex others, female-female pairs maintain closer distances than male-male pairs. Bell et al, also cite other research by Crawford and Unger,2000; Deux and La France, 1998; DePaulo and Friedman, 1998 which state, "findings may reflect stronger female socialization to be affiliative, more experience by females with intimate nonverbal modalities (2001, p. 260). "Interestingly, some research suggests that a woman's point in the menstrual cycle affects the personal space she maintains with opposite-sex others" (Bell et al., 2001, p. 260). Personal space is representative of personalization, so it would appear that personalization does vary with gender. To notice the differences in personalization that is evident among numerous age groups, one merely needs to observe students attending any elementary, middle, or high school. Personalization is reflected in the clothes and shoes one wears, as well as, hairstyles, body art, and piercings. Personalization, which includes perceived choice and personal control, is an important part of self-identity which continues throughout life. "A great deal of research has found that when the social environment fosters perceived choice and personal control, the well-being of the elderly is enhanced" [(cf Rodin, 1986; Rowe and Kahn, 1987; Woodward and Wallston, 1987)], (Bell et al., 2001, p. 425). From the research it is reasonable to state that personalization does indeed vary with status, career, gender, and age.

Place attachment

In nature, there are many different species which exhibit place attachment. A mated pair of Bald Eagles will reuse the same nest year after year. Bell et al. state, "some varieties of salmon migrate hundreds of miles before returning to spawn at the site of their origin. Canada geese mate for life and return to the same nesting place year after year (2001, p. 404). In the southwest, female bats form maternity roosts which can contain hundreds to thousands of bats. Different species of penguins return to the same nesting grounds regardless of the environmental difficulties along the way to their final destination of 'home sweet home'. For individuals, homes offer more than just shelter. Bell et al., cite a 1985 study by Duncan, in which he states homes provide meaning, identity and status. Another 1985 study by Werner, Altman, and Oxley states homes 'structure our social relationships, . . . are centers of regular and predictable events, . . .trigger many memories central to our formative past all of which contribute to a form of psychological bonding with this environment (2001, p. 401). This is what is known as place attachment for humans. Place attachment begins in early childhood and continues throughout our lives; people will form new attachments while either maintaining some attachments and relinquishing older attachments. Sometimes people will form place attachments to an area which they choose to become their gravesite. This gives a new meaning to the phrase "there's no place like home".

Several examples of the entire world as a common. Is a paradigm shift occurring?

There is a common idiom which states "it's a small world, and it gets smaller everyday". This phrase could refer to the entire world as a common which indeed has limited resources. Humanity must not only take a close look at what can be done to ensure there are resources available for future generations, but must take action now to preserve those resources. Countries must stop environmental degradation, and become more responsible. A commitment for research of more sources of renewable energy is necessary so that the exploitation of fossil fuels will cease. Many other worldwide resources are vulnerable to depletion and some of these resources are in a tenuous state. If one considers the numerous worldwide concerns, it is easy to see that unless stronger efforts are made, the resources will not be available for the future. This course, *Environmental Psychology,* has addressed other problematic concerns to include urbanization, pollution, noise, etc. Moreover, this writer proposes the following examples: the oil spill in the Gulf of Mexico, the world problem of black carbon, and mining in the area of Glacier National Park. It has been over 10 weeks since the British Petroleum (BP) disaster in the Gulf of Mexico, and currently there is no foreseeable solution. Oil has already spread to the shores of Texas and has leaked into Lake Pontchartrain, Louisiana causing horrendous environmental damage. Recently, the force of Hurricane Alex compounded the problem even more. Another problem recently brought to the forefront is that of black carbon.

> Increasing concentrations of black carbon have substantially contributed to rapid Arctic warming during the past three decades. A paper from that journal, "Climate response to regional radiative [sic] forcing during the twentieth century," was authored by climate researchers Drew Shindell, at the NASA Goddard Institute for Space Studies, and Greg Faluvegi of Columbia University. Shindell, Faluvegi, and many other climate scientists believe that limiting black carbon sources may "buy the world some time" in the race to control climate change as richer nations develop their climate change policies and begin taking the slow steps towards overhauling their carbon heavy energy sources (Ricciardi, 2009, p.1).

On a positive note, there was a recent victory for the environment due to an agreement signed by the governments of British Colombia and the State of Montana

> to ban all mining and energy development on public lands in the transboundary North Fork of the Flathead River Valley. . . Until now, the river's western and northern slopes -- thousands of acres bordering Glacier National Park-- were slated for mountain-top removal coal mining, gold mining, and oil and gas drilling. Earthjustice and other

conservation groups successfully petitioned the United Nations as well as U.S. and Canadian leaders to protect this spectacularly beautiful wildlife corridor, home to grizzlies, wolves, wolverines, lynx, mountain goat and endangered trout (Presco, 2010, p.1).

This agreement was considered a victory for Earthjustice and is evidence of a paradigm shift which is occurring worldwide. More environmentally conscious groups and organizations are established worldwide in an effort to educate the public, and lobby for legislature to protect precious resources.

The goals of antecedent strategies, and a brief discussion as to whether education is effective.

As per Bell et al., "antecedent strategies precede the behavior they are attempting to change. In many cases the primary targets are attitudes. . . Simply stated, the goal of these strategies is to 'make people care' " (2001, p. 480). Antecedent strategies are methods utilized in attempts to enhance an awareness-level of the public, and in turn, the hope is that behaviors will change accordingly, and people will behave more responsibly in their endeavors at preserving the environment.

Education is only as effective as the target market is receptive and perceptive. "Environmental education involves making people aware of the scope and nature of environmental problems and of behavioral alternatives that might alleviate them. Often, education changes attitudes favorably toward preserving the environment" (Bell et al., 2001, p. 481). However, an education campaign alone is not in itself effective enough to cause behavioral changes. Bell et al., cite several studies regarding the impact of education on attitudes; "in North America and Europe, general concern for the environment is high (e.g., Cohen and Horm-Wingerd, 1993; Dunlap and Mertig, 1995; Wall, 1995), but the relationship between general pro-environmental attitudes and subsequent behavior is somewhat tenuous." (2001, p. 482). For behavior to change, people must acknowledge the fact that change is necessary because the problem impacts their lives in a personal way, and be willing and able to adapt their behaviors. A factor that reinforces education is the method and means of practicing what is learned to make this new behavior a conditioned response. For example, in many larger cities, recycling campaign efforts have been made through the collaborative efforts of the media and numerous agencies; information about cost and effectiveness of recycling was provided to the residents. The residents were provided with separate bins for recycling home products, and separate days for the collection of recyclable items by the Department of Sanitation. The residents were able to acknowledge the need for recycling, and were able to adapt their behavior so that the new behavior is a conditioned response. The residents received positive reinforcement through the community at large for their individual efforts. An awareness of the problem and an education program to resolve the problem is inadequate in dealing with the existing problem; people must have the ways and means to deal with the problem, usually with little or minimal efforts on their part.

Jean-Marie Nixon

What I am doing to save the environment

To change behavior to save the environment, I have raised my children to be consciously aware of the environment, and they have stressed the importance of this to their children, students, and peers accordingly, and support renewable resources. My husband and I live in a small community in the Coconino Forest in Sedona, Arizona (red rock country). We are water conscious, our home is xeriscaped, there is no grass, but instead there are rocks and indigenous plants, so that water usage is minimal. We also collect rain water during the monsoon season. We share our environment with the indigenous animals of the forest, and have a great appreciation of nature (Northern Arizona is home to numerous species of birds, bald eagles, mountain lions, black bears, coyotes, javelinas, deer, elk, bobcats, etc). We must plan our trips (the closest Wal-Mart is approximately 20 miles away, and the closest mall is over an hour away), so that we do not waste fuel or gasoline. Most of the time we travel on our motorcycle to reduce the use of gasoline. We do not purchase many items that must be recycled, but we do recycle when necessary. We cool our home with an evaporative cooler, so we utilize fresh air.

Perhaps the most important plan for the future is not to waste a minute of life and continue to appreciate and enjoy the environment, as well as, continue to preserve what we can for future generations.

References

Bell, P.A., Greene, T.C., Fisher, J.D., Baum, A. (2001). *Environmental psychology* (5th ed.) Belmont, CA: Wadsworth Group/Thomson Learning.

Corey, G., Corey, M.S., Callanan, P. (2003). Introduction to professional ethics. In Julie Martinez Editor *Issues and ethics in the helping profession* (p.13). Pacific Grove: Brooks/Cole.

Presco, T. (2010, February 9). Earth justice [Web post]. Retrieved from http://www.earthjustice.org/features/dazzling-flathead-valley-preserved-from-development.

Ricciardi, M.(2009, May 30). Ecolocalizer [Web post]. Retrieved from http://www.ecolocalizer.com/2009/05/30/limiting-black-soot-and-ozone-%e2%80%93-buying-time.

Taylor, J., (2006). Kick No. 9: Our lady worships the sun. In Lucia Watson Editor *Our lady of weight loss* (p.69). New York: Viking Studio/Penguin Group.

Retrieved from WebMD website: http://SeasonalAffectDisorder(SAD)-causesandriskfactorswww.webmd.com/depression/tc/seasonal-affect-disorder-sad-topic-overview

Chapter 3

Thoughts on the hazards of counseling

Is counseling a "hazardous" profession? Steps the counselor can take to minimize stress and maintain vitality.

Those who choose to enter the counseling profession need to have a strong sense of self, or rather their person, their inner being. Many individuals enter into helping professions, while retaining "unfinished or unresolved" business. Upon graduation, it does not take very long to go from being an idealistic classroom student who is ready to take on specific societal challenges to being a tired, harried, public servant suffering from vicarious traumatization, and burnout (both hazards of fieldwork). However, if one remains dedicated to their original goal upon entering the profession (of assisting others), cognizant of their limitations, and constantly utilizes the existing support network of colleagues and loved ones, one can continue to do meaningful, important work in assisting others in times of need.

I, Jean-Marie Nixon, have often used the following analogy in working with interns and students – it is important to remember that you are the instrument, or rather tool of the trade. If you were a musician, you would keep your instrument finely tuned, whether it is new strings, reeds, etc; if you were a contractor, you would keep your tools clean, and sharpened. As a counselor, advocate, case manager, etc, you are the tool; you must keep your mind sharp and focused. To do this, you must take time for your own needs, for if you are not aware of self, and possible or potential burnout issues, then you cannot help others. Helping others is the primary goal of this profession.

Self awareness is a key factor in remaining focused on the goal of helping others. As one works with other individuals, couples, and families, etc. in resolving their intimate issues, and immediate crisis, one has great power along with great responsibility to the clients. Those with "unfinished needs" will not be able to adequately help others in striving to attain their goals – they will invariably work towards their own "unfinished needs". At these times, it is important to remember one's initial ideals and motivations for entering the helping profession, as well as, being truly honest and meta-cognizant regarding personal issues, fears, conflicts, etc. Counselors, who are unaware or even aware and uncomfortable of their own inner conflicts, may consciously or unconsciously, avoid helping clients in these areas. They may "steer" clients away from certain issues. For example, a counselor who has come from an alcoholic and abusive home may not wish to address these issues with clients from similar backgrounds. It may be too painful for the therapist, and the therapist may be unaware of how their personal life is influencing their work with others. As previously stated, it is important to be meta-cognizant of one's' self. It is necessary to remember your academics and the internalization of one's accepted theory of practice. It is also vital to hone the skills, and techniques learned in training, so that you can 'get past' one's bias, fears, etc. Another important reminder is that the clients have the power within themselves for adequate and substantial change. The client needs to be part of the problem solving process. In creating a "plan of action", both clients and counselor need to be participants. There are 2 major reasons for this: (1) people will generally support what they help to create. The client must be able to "buy in" to the process. Counseling and therapy is hard work, involving intimate levels of painful emotions. The client will not remain committed to working through the pain if they are not committed to the plan. (2) The counselor is in a powerful position. It is very easy for the counselor to postulate and ponder "if the client would just do as I say, the client would have an easier time, or everything will work out if the client would simply follow the plan. If the counselor abuses their power, the client will not be empowered. The client has the power within to change, it is the counselor, who helps by drawing out what has been 'buried within' the client, so that the client has Hope, and can see the possibility of change, and work towards that goal. This can work with either short-term or long-term goals. But it is vital to working with clients who have long-term goals, as one's changing needs require updates to a working plan. Sometimes, the client "just wants the problem fixed" and doesn't see that they have an active part in the problem solving process (this is more common with family work). This resistance can act as another stressor for the counselor, especially if the counselor has become too attached, or to close to the problem.

As one works with clients, there are numerous stressors that come into being, beyond the presenting factors. One will find that clients will want to rely more on the counselor for "everyday unidentified stressful events". The client will think their emergencies are your emergencies. It is easy for them to call the counselor (and easy for the counselor to be caught up in a dependency situation) and be "talked through the problem", rather than the client review the plan in their mind, and go through the problem solving process on their own. Therefore, these everyday occurrences will continue to happen and it is necessary for the client to work through the plan. The client must relearn or teach themselves, thereby making and reinforcing new synaptic responses, and utilizing neurotransmitters sufficiently, so the client is positively reinforced physically, mentally, and emotionally.

It is important to remember that the client's behavior is not your behavior; you are not 'on call' 24-7. Make sure you are discussing your concerns with your supervisor(s) either through clinical supervision, during you own sessions, or case specific staff meetings. Sharing your concerns with other professionals will help to reassure young professionals that: (1) they are not alone in this process of helping others (they are not the only professional in helping specific clients, as the client may see a staff psychiatrist, psychologist, nurse for medication, advocate, agency worker, etc), (2) sharing will serve as a reminder of why this is their chosen profession (Nixon's note -- because though the work itself can be tiresome, difficult, and extremely challenging, it is also possibly the most rewarding work one can ever hope to do), and (3) provide other sources or avenues for treatment possibilities. There may be times during one's day when "you are not 'doing therapy', but what you are doing is very therapeutic.

Lastly, it is important, vital, and necessary to keep one's life balanced. Remember that you still need some alone time to "de-stress" (this could be through time at the gym, an exercise or yoga class), but you are not alone, spend time with your friends, family, loved ones. These are the important people in your life, the people to whom you come home, the people you love and who love you. This balance will help you maintain your own wellness, spirituality, health, and mental clarity. In helping yourself, you help others; and in looking for the good in others, you find the best in yourself.

Values -- Is it possible for counselors to keep their values out of their counseling sessions?

Values – it is said that the only thing a person can truly call their own is their values and you take your values to the grave. To imagine that one will work without reflecting on their values is a lesson in futility. One's value system is engrained and necessary, just as breathing, but also, as with other vital requirements, our value system will also evolve, if we are open-minded and tolerant. In the text, Issues and Ethics in the Helping Profession, Corey, Corey, and Callanan state: "Research has shown that counselors' values influence every phase of the therapeutic process. . . Clients are influenced by therapists' values and often adopt some of these values . . . In our view it is neither possible nor desirable for counselors to be completely neutral in this respect" (2003, p. 72). Granted, there are counselors who practice at the extreme ends of this spectrum. Some may almost impose their values when working with clients, while others attempt to keep their values hidden, so as not to influence the clients. Other types of counselors, religious, or spiritual such as priests, ministers, rabbis, work to guide the clients, and influence them along the values, and teachings of a specific faith.

Nixon's note: The ethical concerns of this profession must be for the good of the client, as well as the counselor, and any involved agencies. By this, I mean that prior to accepting an individual or family as a client(s), the counselor must be aware of any personal bias, attitude, or value system, which may have bearing on the treatment plan. If the counselor is personally involved with friends or family members of the prospective client, it is important to discuss the situation with a supervisor (prior to accepting the client) to avoid any possible mishandling of the treatment plan.

Working with clients from diverse backgrounds, will afford one the opportunity to witness various value systems. Although the therapist, may not agree with clients' value system, it is vital to be genuine, empathic, and have a positive regard with clients; one should not be judgmental; it is not the counselor's place to prosthelytize, that type of work is better suited to the clergy. While maintaining genuineness, one should be aware of the non-verbal messages that are reflected to the client, as it is possible to display feelings without verbal statements. The counselor should always remember that they are in the "power position", and their words and actions have great impact on the clients.

There are a few exceptions to this guideline; clients whose values and beliefs are illegal, hurtful to children, the infirm, or the elderly, and those which contribute to delinquency and deviancy should be addressed for remediation (this is most common in mandatory court appointed clients). It is at times such as these, when the counselor's value system and the client's value system are incongruent, that the counselor may then experience inner turmoil. If the counselor cannot maintain objective neutrality, remain genuine, and have a positive regard to the client, it is ethical and necessary to discuss the situation with a supervisor. It is also important to keep your notes and documentation neutral (subjective, objective, assessment, and plan [SOAP] notes). This type of record keeping may be best for documentation; especially when dealing with third parties, such as other agencies (city, county, or state, the court system, insurance companies, etc). During the instances when the counselor's values clash with the clients – this is the time for the counselor to look within, be meta-cognitive, and self-explore as to whether or not it is necessary to have similar values in order to accomplish effective, productive work with clients. If the counselor can remain genuine, tolerant, and perhaps utilize various techniques from their theory of practice, the counselor may indeed help the client to help themselves; which is the goal of the profession.   On the other hand, if one recognizes and acknowledges their limitations (I applaud those that do), and comes to the realization that they cannot genuinely assist the client due to a clash of values, and the counselor cannot function effectively, the counselor must consult with others on the need for referral. It is unethical to continue to work with clients in this situation.

Counselors, therapists, interns, and students in this field, who remain open-minded, and tolerant, may discover interesting personal and group dynamics while working with diverse populations. The exploration of another's value system can be a glimpse into deep intimate memories and moments.

Clients offer the counselor a unique privilege and opportunity when they ask a member of our profession for help. We in the helping profession should do all we can to maintain this level of trust by being ethical, genuine, empathic, and offering unconditional positive regard.

Informed consent: a basic right of clients, and the three elements involved in adequate informed consent.

Here in the United States, it is general knowledge that individuals have the basic right to life, liberty, and the pursuit of happiness, but with rights also come responsibilities. In the helping profession, we are offered a unique responsibility when clients face their fears, build up their courage, and ask for help (often times in the pursuit of their happiness). The counselor must ensure that clients are educated of their rights regarding treatment plans (benefits, risks, short and long term goals, options or alternatives to treatment plans (individual or group therapy). Clients need also be aware of confidentiality and privilege, as well as, exceptions to confidentiality. It is important that the clients understand these rights, and then after careful consideration, they can decide to give independent, autonomous informed consent.

The process of informed consent involves guiding the client through every step of the procedures. The counselor or another staff member explains the initial screening and intake procedures (collecting background information can be stressful for clients), prior to gathering the necessary information to make a diagnosis; this can be done in a manner so that the client is capable of understanding what will occur. The client is then able to review the questions, give feedback, and ask questions of their own. The client should be provided with information regarding treatment options; depending on the diagnosis, the treatment options may vary from a few classes (parenting, DUI, etc), individual or group therapy with a facilitator, counselor, or psychologist, or perhaps even meeting regularly with a staff psychiatrist for medical treatment, along with regular follow up visits with a nurse. Treatment options or alternatives vary depending on client needs and insurance company protocol. When the clients are involved throughout the process, the clients are more educated, able to understand and give consent, and thereby become more willing participants in their treatment program. This is the purpose of informed consent and it is the ethical responsibility of each mental health care provider to ensure the clients have the right of informed consent.

Throughout the process of informed consent, it is also the responsibility of the helping professional to ensure the legal aspects of informed consent are met; there are three elements necessary to fulfill this requirement: capacity, comprehension of information, and voluntariness.

The client must have the capacity to understand, is able to comprehend, and is a voluntarily participant. Individuals with capacity are able to make rationally sound choices and decisions for themselves. The ability to comprehend means the clients understand the reasons for their involvement in the treatment process, have an understanding of what to expect throughout the process, and have knowledge of the benefits, and risks involved with the therapeutic process. It is important that their involvement be voluntary -- that they are there as willing participants (this does not apply to court mandated cases), and that they know that anytime they may desire, they can make a choice to withdraw from their treatment plan.

If a client does not have the mental capacity to understand, cannot comprehend the treatment process, and is not a willing, voluntary participant the professional cannot ethically provide services to the individual (again this does not apply to mandatory, court ordered cases).

When the professional and the client have thoroughly discussed the right of informed consent, and the client is aware, and involved with the process; then the client has been, and continues to be part of their treatment plan. Then from a legal perspective will the required three elements have been met. This process allows for the client to be empowered and fully vested in the process. This will allow for maximum progress, growth, and a successful outcome for all parties.

Chapter 4

Thoughts on working with groups

Confidentiality

Group work allows its members to witness that they are not alone in their situations, as others are going through similar thoughts, situations, feelings, etc. As such, group work can be very powerful for its' members – being in the group can help promote feelings of self-efficacy and empowerment. On the other hand, group work can also have an adverse effect due to the fact that members may feel that they are at risk by being in a group where their individual confidences are not respected.

Confidentiality is necessary and vital for quality, effective work; otherwise, a group will merely "go through the motions"; sit, greet each other, share light conversation, but nothing of real matter; they will not get to the reasons for their involvement in the group. If the group members do not feel that they are in a confidential arena, they will not feel "safe", nor will they disclose the nature or reasons that they are in the group, be it voluntary or mandatory. A group setting for some can be very intimidating, especially to those that have not been involved in group counseling. It is one thing to share private matters with the counselor, but quite another thing to share the same feelings, matters, and experiences with strangers.

It is up to the counselor or group facilitator to stress the importance of confidentiality from the early pre-screening, information gathering, intakes, evaluations, etc on through the initial meeting, as well as throughout the duration of the group (at regular times this should be restricted, and participants reminded of the group policies – what happens in the group, stays in the group). It is vital to stress that while it is impossible to ensure that others will respect the confidences of the other members, the facilitator can be a model. The members can see that the leader takes this issue to heart and they should likewise, follow that path. The facilitator can have the members sign a confidentiality agreement, and the group can discuss the option of some type of sanction if the confidentiality is broken. By making the members part of the creation process, they are then more willing to support the group process.

The members should also be informed of the limits and exceptions to confidentiality. The facilitator should stress that each individual is responsible for keeping the confidences of the group. But the exception applies to the concept of clear and imminent danger to the client or others; or if legal requirements demand the information is revealed. The facilitator is ethically bound to discuss the matter with other professionals when in doubt of the validity of the exception (Corey, 2004, p. 61).

Group members need to be told that each state has unique laws and statutes regarding confidential nature, and in general, legal privilege does not apply to group treatment. "Counselors are legally required to report clients' threats to harm themselves or others. This covers cases of child abuse or neglect, incest, or child molestation" (Corey, 2004, p.61). It is always better to be open and inform the group members if and when the facilitator must break confidentiality, rather than hide the fact. By the facilitator being open, the group is more likely to be cooperative and hopefully, somewhat understanding; perhaps not receptive, but more aware and realistic of the situation.

Cohesion and productivity

Cohesion – the unity and solidarity of a group begins to develop in the early stages of group work; however, it is vital to the working stage of the group. In the working stage, trust has been established, negative feelings have been brought to the surface, and initial conflicts have been resolved. The group has worked as a team, been able to support what they have created, and in doing so have become cohesive. If the cohesion is well established, the members

> have taken risks and have been positively reinforced; now they realize that conflict can occur and be resolved, and it is okay to allow further trust and continue group interaction. Because cohesion has developed, the members can "open up" on a deeper level, share painful experiences, and with the help of one other, work through the experience. When other members witness this struggle of pain, it binds them to each other. The cohesion then provides motivation for progress and this is necessary for the group's success.

If the members do not develop a "sense of groupness", the members will remain fragmented, they will merely "go through the motions" of group work – individuals will remain locked within their ego defense mechanisms -- their fear and mistrust will fester locked behind the walls in their minds. Group cohesiveness occurs through commitment by the members and facilitator – the members take the necessary steps to commit to themselves and each other to do the hard work of the group.

Yalom (1995) maintains that cohesion is a strong determinant of a positive group outcome. If members experience little sense of belonging . . . there is little likelihood that they will benefit, and they may well experience negative outcomes . . .groups with a here-and-now focus are almost invariably vital and cohesive. In contrast, groups in which members merely talk about issues with a "there-and-then" focus rarely develop much cohesion (Corey, 2004, p. 108).

Because cohesion has developed, other factors merge into the group process. Members are more willing to trust. **Trust** manifests into **acceptance** – members are more open to risk-taking, sharing deep emotions (often very painful) without fear of judgment or rejection.

The participants can be **empathic and caring** with each other. The members realize that although they are different, they have much in common with each other. The establishment of empathy and caring in the group leads to expressions of intimacy (individuals wants, dreams, and desires for their lives).

In the verbalization of genuine **intimacy** comes the idea of **hope.** Change cannot occur until the participants believe that change is possible – that there is hope. Hope in itself is therapeutic, because it motivates people to explore methods for change, as well as, insight to the possibility of making new and different choices for their lives. They no longer have to think "well, I made this bed and now I have to sleep in it" – they can see that at a point in their past, they made a choice/s, but the choice/s did not have the desired outcome and now they can give themselves permission to make other, new, and different choices. Hope in itself can be liberating, even if only for a short time. Hope allows the members to visualize an alternate future, which results in **freedom to plan and experiment** – to verbalize the plans, fears, etc. with the group. While in the group, the members can "walk the idea through their head" – the group can be a supportive sounding board.

This can further lead to a **cathartic expression of "pent-up feelings".** This **disclosure** is vital to an individual's progress within the group. The group members in turn are positively reinforced by witnessing the individual's **commitment to change,** as well as, the individual's hard work and progress, and in turn, the members are further motivated by their own hope to make similar strides to reach their individual goals. The group is supportive in reaching the goals via **confrontation and feedback** in a caring, straight forward, and affirming manner.

A description of the ABC theory of REBT.

The ABC theory – people have an Activating event in their lives "A", to which they have some type of Belief "B" which results in an emotional Consequence "C". Individuals put themselves into certain situations by their "Beliefs: about certain events. It is this belief system that creates the consequence (not the activating event).

Activating event →   A

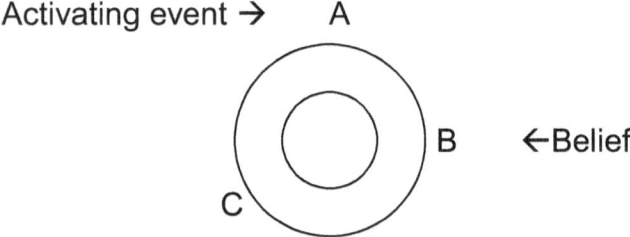

B   ←Belief

C

Consequence (emotional) →

The goals of REBT involve acceptance – the counselor assists the members to accept themselves via an unconditional self-acceptance,

(USA) and unconditional other acceptance (UOA), along with an awareness and internalization of how these two (USA and UOA) are interrelated. Once the individual group members are able to accept themselves, they can then accept others. Clients are taught that they alone own their emotional reactions – they have an internal locus of control. Therefore, in ownership, they are no longer the victims of an external locus of control. Clients are taught to pay attention to self-talk thus enabling themselves to alter their belief system and develop a healthier phenomenological approach. The client must be willing to do the necessary work to make positive change – in order to change their world; they must first change their thoughts.

The origins for faulty thinking often develop in childhood when children develop ideas of "should", "must", "ought"—the child then associates these ideas with love, acceptance, and approval of others. These ideas are then further reinforced (positively or negatively) through Activating events → Beliefs → emotional Consequence. Despite the fact that as children, clients were not equipped to question and challenge these beliefs; as adults, they can now be aware of negative and self-destructive thought patterns and thus learn to make changes for new "beliefs" and thoughts, and thereby change their lives.

Irrational beliefs are confronted by teaching the ABCs, challenging the beliefs system, teaching positive self-talk. After the clients have grasped these new ideas, other methods are utilized to continue growth – these include USA, "vivid imagery" (what I refer to as "paint me a picture"), humor, attacking shame, and role-playing.

The role of self-rating is important – it challenges one to detoxify oneself of crippling beliefs, oftentimes associated with long-term guilt, and empowers one to look at new, alternate avenues of positive, healthy self-awareness and self-confidence to maintain an internal locus of control.

References

Corey, G., Corey, M.S., Callanan, P. (2003). In Julie Martinez Editor *Issues and ethics in the helping profession*. Pacific Grove: Brooks/Cole.

Chapter 5

Thoughts regarding assessments and testing

Norms: development and importance

The science of psychology is closely intertwined with the sciences of sociology, personalities, the environment, etc. These sciences and technologies are related through the work that is predicted, affected, and established through the study of the behaviors of mankind as a social animal. Throughout history, social mores and group norms come into place and are important because the existence of norms assist in maintaining order and structure. In this instance, social norms are rules (the rules or norms can be explicit, implicit, descriptive, etc.) that a group of people acknowledges for acceptable or unacceptable behaviors, beliefs, or attitudes, etc.

It is from this base that the human relations training movement has sought to increase social and psychological interactions among different peoples and to foster understanding of situations . . . However, it has also been determined that larger social group norms heavily influence individual behavior, regardless of individual personality characteristics or individual life experience. . . a person would alter his or her behavior if it ran contrary to group norms (Axelson, 1999, p. 181).

In the field of psychology, most of the things which are studied are tested. One develops hypothesis and then does further testing to determine correlations and findings. In the scope of their textbook, *Psychological testing*, the authors Anne Anastasi, and Susana Urbina, further explore the concept of norms in statistics and testing.

Most of the things we measure in psychology tend to have about both number of

> cases on both sides of the middle. . . most distributions are approximately symmetrical . . . the standard of comparison is the bell-shaped curve that is widely approximated in psychological research . . . It is called the normal curve. . (Aron and Aron, 1999, p. 20).

In the area of psychological testing, the development and use of norms are necessary tools utilized to interpret test scores. "Scores on psychological tests are most commonly interpreted by reference to *norms* that represent the test performance of the standard sample. The norms are thus empirically established by determining what persons in a representative group actually do on the test (Anastasi and Urbina, 1997, p. 48). There are two types of norms: developmental norms and within group norms.

Developmental norms are used to attach meaning to test scores in order to demonstrate whether or not the individual is progressing along the normal developmental path. These can be used to describe mental age capacity of an individual at the time of the test.

> However expressed, scores based on developmental norms tend to be psychometrically crude and do not lend themselves well to precise statistical treatment. Nevertheless, they have considerable appeal for descriptive purposes, especially in the intensive clinically study of individuals and for certain research purposes (Anastasi and Urbina, 1997, pp. 54-55).

The use of developmental norms has also led to research in child psychology with the use of ordinal scales. The scales compare the child's current development in major areas with typical behavior development at certain ages. These scales are tools utilized for standardized measurements and tests. Most tests include within-group norms. "With such norms, the individual's performance is evaluated in terms of the performance of the most nearly comparable standardization group, as when comparing a child's raw score with that of children of the same chronological age or . . . school grade" (Anastasi and Urbina, 1997, p. 58). For analysis purposes, the within-group scores provide a consistent measurement.

It is important to note that the names of the tests should be included with the individuals' scores. Otherwise, the scores cannot be properly interpreted. Without proper interpretation the relativity of norms is mute as individuals may have taken different tests altogether.

> Any norm, however, expressed, is restricted to the particular normative population from which it was derived. The test user should never lose sight of the way in which norms are established. Psychological test norms are in no sense absolute, universal, or permanent. They merely represent the test performance of the persons constituting the standardization sample (Anastasi and Urbina, 1997, p. 68).

Norms serve specific purposes in the areas of assessments, testing, and statistics. They are tools used in research, education and training, etc. However, they do not represent the unlimited potential of the individuals being tests or assessed. As professionals in the helping field it is important to remember to focus on individuals rather than numbers.

References

Anastasi, A., and Urbina, S. (1997). Norms and the meaning of test scores. In Janzow, P. Editor, *Psychological testing* (pp. 48 – 83). Upper Saddle River, NJ: Prentice Hall.

Aron, A., and Aron, E.N. (1999). Displaying the order in a group of numbers. In Roberts, N. Editor, *Statistics for psychology* (p. 20). Upper Saddle River, NJ: Prentice Hall.

Axelson, J.A., (1999). Social political issues. In Murphy, E. Editor, *Counseling and development in a multicultural society* (p. 181). Pacific Grove, CA: Brooks/Cole.

I.Q. -- fixed and unchanging -- the heritability and modifiability of intelligence

As per Anne Anastasi and Susana Urbina, in their textbook, *Psychological Testing,* "an IQ is an expression of an individual's ability level at a given point in time, in relation to the available age norms" (1999, p. 295). It is important to take note of the fact that this measurement is similar to a snapshot in time – it exists for this moment, because it is not fixed and unchanging, but rather ever-changing.

> A . . . point to bear in mind is that intelligence is not a single, unitary ability, but a composite of several functions. The term is commonly used to cover that combination of abilities required for survival and advancement within a particular culture (Anastasi, 1986c). It follows that the specific abilities included in this composite, as well as their relative weights, vary with time and place (Anastasi and Urbina, 1999, p. 296).

In her textbook, *The Psychology of Aging: Theory, Research, and Interventions*, author, Janet Belsky indicates the nervous system is 'plastic', as research shows findings that dendrites grow to compensate for age-related neuron loss (1999, p. 85). In addition, Belsky surmises the main message of the cognitive remediation studies is that you can improve IQ in later life – within limits (1999, p. 192). However, in so far as testing, the problem with giving traditional IQ tests to measure intelligence in adult life is that the IQ test was constructed to measure success in school (Belsky, 1999, p. 176). "One's relative ability tends to increase with age in those functions whose value is emphasized by one's culture or subculture; and one's relative ability tends to decrease in those functions whose value is deemphasized (Anastasi and Urbina, 1999, p. 296). Life experiences contribute to practicality, and common sense should not be underestimated (or as some people say, don't outsmart your common sense"). "There are many important psychological functions that intelligence tests have never undertaken to measure. Mechanical, motor, musical, and artistic aptitudes are obvious examples. Motivational, emotional, and attitudinal variables are important determiners of achievement in all areas" [sic] (Anastasi and Urbina, 1999, p. 296). It is reasonable to acknowledge that a person's IQ is not fixed and unchanging, but grows and evolves as does the individual.

There is currently considerable uncertainty and disagreement regarding the contribution of heritability and modifiability of intelligence.

> A major source of controversy pertains to the interpretation of heritability estimates. Specifically, a heritability index shows the proportional contribution of genetic or hereditary factors to the total variance of a particular trait in a given population under

existing conditions (Anastasi and Urbina, 1999, p. 297).

Other factors to consider are those regarding modifiability; the impact of environment, culture, diet, and lifestyle.

Heritability indexes have been computed by various formulas . . . but their basic data are measures of familial resemblance in the trait under consideration. Apart from questionable data, heritability indexes have other intrinsic limitations. . . First, the concept of heritability is applicable to populations, not individuals. . . Second, heritability indexes refer to the population on which they were found at the time. Any change in either heritability or environmental conditions would alter the heritability index. . .Third, heritability does not indicate the degree of modifiability of a trait. Even if the heritability index of a trait in a given population is 100%, it does not follow that the contribution of environment to that trait is unimportant. . . regardless of the magnitude of heritability indexes found for IQs in various populations, one empirical fact is well established: The IQ is not fixed and unchanging; and it is amenable to modification by environmental interventions (Anastasi and Urbina, 1999, pp. 297-298).

There are many factors which contribute to intelligence, none of which should be discounted. In addition to culture, lifestyle, and environment, it should be noted that personal motivation, positive reinforcement, and the satisfaction in the joy of learning and mastering of skills all contribute to the lifelong learning cycle.

References

Anastasi, A., & Urbina, S. (1997). Nature of intelligence. In Janzow, P. Editor, *Psychological testing* (pp. 48 – 83). Upper Saddle River, NJ: Prentice Hall.

Belsky, J. (1999). Aging in action. Enhancing wisdom. New conceptions and tests of adult intelligence. In Brace-Thompson, J. Editor, *Psychology of adult development and aging* (pp. 85, 192, 176). Pacific Grove, CA: Brooks/Cole.

Confidentiality in testing

The concerns of confidentiality in the helping profession have always been of importance. By the very nature of the work, the professional is entrusted and ethically bound to protect and ensure the safety of the client's inner most cognitive thought processes, familial background and history, as well as, diagnosis of various types. Clients must be informed of the limits and exceptions to confidentiality. The exception applies to the concept of clear and imminent danger to the client or others; or if legal requirements demand the information is revealed. The professional is ethically bound to discuss the matter with other colleagues when in doubt of the validity of the exception (Corey, 2004, p. 61). Clients need to be told that each state has unique laws and statutes regarding confidential nature, and it is always better to be open and inform the client if and when the professional must break confidentiality. This applies not only to the role of counseling, but also to the area of testing (as many clients will undergo intake assessments, and be involved with other tests or diagnostic procedures). "The fundamental question is: Who shall have access to test results? Several considerations influence the answer in particular situations. . . the security of test content, the hazards of misunderstanding test scores, and the need for various persons to know the results" (Anastasi, and Urbina, 1999, p. 542). It is widely accepted that individuals have the right to their own test results, and in the case of minors, the parents and/or legal guardians should also have access to this information. Be that as it may, interpretations and findings should be easy to understand, in lay terms and not 'technical jargon', and concise and to the point in regards to the purpose of the test(s).

> Discussions of the confidentiality of test records have usually dealt with accessibility to a *third* person, other than the individual tested (or parent of a minor) and the examiner. The underlying principle is that such records should *not* be released without the knowledge and consent of the test taker, unless such a release is mandated by law or permitted by law for valid purposes (Anastasi and Urbina, 1999, p. 542).

When individuals are tested in educational, legal, health, or employment settings, the individuals should be informed of the who, why, when, where, and how of the situation as it pertains to the information, circumstances, and any other pertinent criteria regarding the test(s). As with other areas in the helping profession, there is documentation, as well as, agencies and committees which oversee the ethics of the profession. These include but are not limited to Statement on the Disclosure of Test Data, the Statement on Record Keeping Guidelines, and the American Psychologists Association's Committee on Legal Issues. When in doubt or confronted with an ethical dilemma which involves areas of confidentiality, it is of vital importance that the helping professional keep in mind this thought "am I doing what is best for my client".

Author's note: you have to be able to face the person in the mirror every morning.

References

Anastasi, A., and Urbina, S. (1997). Ethical and social considerations in testing. In Janzow, P. Editor, *Psychological testing* (pp. 48 – 83). Upper Saddle River, NJ: Prentice Hall.

Corey, G., (2004). Ethical and professional issues in group practice. In Gebo, L. Editor, Theory and practice of group counseling (p. 61). Belmont, CA: Brooks/Cole.

ABOUT THE AUTHOR

Jean-Marie Nixon, the daughter of Earl Vernon and Mary Louise Mills, is a native Texan. She divides her time between her hometown of San Antonio, Texas and the home she shares with her loving husband, Patrick E. Nixon, in Sedona, Arizona. She is a proud mother and grandmother. She is also a successful business woman, and is the CEO of "Turn the Other Cheek". She enjoys motorcycle riding with her husband, traveling, karaoke, and dancing, as well as, sewing, cooking, reading, and spending time with friends and family.

She holds multiple degrees; she received her master's degree in psychology from California Coast University. She had a fulfilling, challenging, and rewarding career with child protective services in the State of Delaware. She has also worked in the field of child and family case management, and has provided services for families in crisis in the State of Arizona. She has collaborated with numerous agencies to include Family Court, Juvenile Probation, Child Mental Health, Catholic Charities, the Boys & Girls Club, Girl Scouts of America, and various foster care agencies. This is her first book.

www.ingramcontent.com/pod-product-compliance
Lightning Source LLC
Chambersburg PA
CBHW022252290526
45785CB00015B/722